The Power of Purity

Freedom from the Roots of Sexual Sin

Tony Ingrassia

ISBN # 0-9747007-0-3

For more information contact:
    Tony Ingrassia at **tony@powerofpurity.org**

The Power of Purity

Freedom from the Roots of Sexual Sin

Table of Contents

PART 1

FOUNDATIONS

SEXUAL PURITY?

God makes it very clear in the Bible that His standard for our lives is sexual purity. Yet many Christian men struggle deeply with the sexual area of their lives. Typically, our problem is not that we don't know what is right or wrong. We have plenty of head knowledge. The problem is our ability to do the right thing. In spite of what we know, many of us continue to struggle deeply with, among other things, wandering eyes, lust-filled hearts, compulsive masturbation, and various forms of pornography, including magazines, videos, television, and the Internet. For many of us, a kind of silent resignation to defeat eventually comes to define our lives as we sequence endlessly through the familiar cycle of failure, guilt, shame, renewed determination, promises to God, ongoing struggle, and back to failure. Is this as good as it gets? Is this what God intended when He made us more than conquerors and gave us all things that pertain to life and godliness? Is true sexual purity really possible for the average Christian guy? In this section we will come to understand clearer than ever before God's standard of sexual purity for our lives, and then discover the only way sexual purity can ever be achieved. If we are to ever truly honor God with our sexuality, not just on the outside — what we do, where we go, what we touch, what we look at, and what we say — but also on the inside — what we think about, our desires, and the energy and motives that live in our hearts — we will need to have a radical experience with God in which He does something for us that we could never do for ourselves. The good news is that we serve a God who is willing and able to radically change our lives from the inside out if we get serious about doing business with Him. I know, because that's what He did for me!

CHAPTER 1

CALLING ALL
PERVERTS...NOT!

Why Sex?

Come on, gentlemen! You already know why we need to talk about sex: because sex is central to masculinity, and sex represents one of the most common and deepest struggles for many Christian men. Consider the following examples from the lives of average men I've spoken with recently.

Note: all names have been changed to protect the guilty!

> Doug struggles deeply with frequent masturbation. He wishes he could stop and lives in the shadow of secret shame because of his actions. He said he considers his habit a kind of unfaithfulness to his wife, but is simply powerless to change his behavior.

> Mark said he has a crazy sexual history. Before he got married he was on the constant prowl and had sex with dozens of different women. Only 4 months after he got married he felt trapped and suffocated as he realized he could only have sex with one woman — his wife — for the rest of his life. He struggles deeply with the constant temptation to seek out other women, and said if it wasn't for the kids, there is no doubt in his mind he would have left his wife long ago.

Tom struggles with Internet pornography. He uses his computer every day and tries to resist the constant temptation that is only a couple mouse clicks away. His wife recently caught him "looking" and he got in big trouble.

John is the pastor of a large church, and his relationship with his wife hasn't had much "sizzle" in a long time. He travels frequently — to do God's work — and confessed he surrenders often to the temptation to watch pornographic movies while alone in his hotel room.

Joe is a missionary in a foreign country. He is serving God full-time, and his ministry is growing and being blessed remarkably. When I shared the story of my sexual struggle with him, he broke down in tears and begged me to help him. He confessed, among several other things, struggling with sexual temptation toward the children around him.

These men are not perverts. They are not sick sexual deviants or sexual predators. I don't even think they represent the "exception to the rule" in the Christian community. They are just regular Christian guys like you and me. I believe every one of them sincerely loves God and wants to serve Him. Each sincerely wants to do the right thing, yet each struggles deeply in various ways with honoring God from the center of his sexuality. This book is not intended to help sexual perverts. It's intended to speak into the hearts of real men about real sex. It's intended for men like those mentioned above, and men like you and me.

Maximum Glory

As Christian men, we are called to bring honor and glory to God through our lives. In fact, the Bible teaches there is a great cosmic conflict literally raging all around us every single day. God Himself is fighting to redeem broken lives and restore them to Himself — to the place of intimacy and fellowship that will empower those once-broken lives to instead bring Him great honor and glory. Satan is fighting to destroy those very same lives and pull them forever from the hand of God. It's a conflict of good versus evil, and one in which the forces of heaven are arrayed against the forces of hell in an immense struggle over the life of each living soul. It's a kind of spiritual chess match, and each person born on planet Earth — including you and me — is a pawn in the game. The enemy knows he cannot overthrow heaven and the throne of God through the direct assault of his power. He already tried that in eternity past when he rallied one-third of the heavenly hosts to his side in his vain attempt to conquer heaven and steal the glory of God. As a result he was cast to the earth (Revelation 12:7-9) and has since adopted a new strategy in his attempt to harm the heart of God. It's as if the devil determined, "Since I cannot destroy God Himself, I will destroy God's creation. I will destroy what God loves the most. I will destroy human lives!" This is not a cosmic fairy tale. It is reality, and it has everything to do with your life and your sexuality. You ask how? Because if it's really true that there is a cosmic conflict being waged over your very life, then the implications of the entirety of your life have serious consequences upon the Kingdom of God. In short, any area of your life that is not completely bringing honor and glory to God is profoundly significant to the battle being waged over your life. God is fighting to capture more of your heart and life in His attempt to align your life with His purposes and His kingdom. The enemy is fighting to hold you in places of sin, autonomy, and bondage that will continue to prohibit your ability to bring glory to God. God wants maximum glory from your life, and Satan wants maximum destruction.

In view of this grand cosmic conflict, I believe it would serve us well to contemplate how our lives can bring the greatest glory to God, and in view of such a question I would like to propose a suggestion. I believe the greatest way we can bring glory to God through our lives is when we learn to bring Him glory through the most broken areas of our lives. The Apostle Paul wrote, "My grace is sufficient for you, for my power is made perfect in weakness. Therefore I will boast all the more gladly about my weaknesses, so that Christ's power may rest on me" (II Corinthians 12:9). It seems the power of God is most evident in our lives not through our strengths and abilities, but through our weaknesses. God gets the greatest glory when through His power He enables us to overcome our weaknesses. This is because anybody who knows us, and how we used to be, knows it isn't because of ourselves that our lives have been changed; it can only be because of God alone, and therefore God alone gets all the glory.

If I don't drink alcohol for 3 years, it's not really any big deal, because I don't have a drinking problem and I don't like to drink alcohol anyway. However, if a raging alcoholic who lost everything because of his alcoholism came to the place through the work of God in his life where he didn't take a drink for 3 years, it would be a completely different matter. God would get a radical level of glory from that man's sobriety because of the corresponding level of radical destruction that previously existed in that man's life. For the alcoholic to learn to honor God with his drinking — or better said his not drinking — the very area of his life where he had dishonored God for so long, God surely would receive maximum glory. In much the same way, I believe God receives tremendous glory — and the devil receives tremendous insult — when we learn to honor Him in the very areas of our lives where we have dishonored Him for so long. Surely God receives glory when we honor Him with our finances. Surely God receives glory when we honor Him with our business affairs. Surely God receives glory when we are the kind of fathers and husbands He has called us to be. God receives glory when we participate faithfully in our church, when we share the gospel with another person, and when we read our Bible or pray. There are so many ways we can bring glory to God and reproach upon the enemy when we honor God with our lives. But the way to bring the *greatest* glory to God is when we learn to bring Him glory from the very places we have failed and dishonored Him for so long in the past, and I believe for most men this includes their sexuality. Imagine it…imagine how magnificent it would be…how much distress it would bring to the enemy and how much glory it would bring to God if we as Christian men could truly honor God completely with our sexuality. That would be maximum glory!

Maximum Destruction

I know it's possible to be a Christian and to still struggle deeply with your sexuality, because that's exactly what I did for over 20 years. In fact, my sexuality was the primary vehicle the enemy used in his attempt to literally destroy everything of significance in my life, including my marriage, my family, my finances, my ministry, my testimony, and my very life. Although I became a Christian when I was 16 years old, and although I sincerely loved God and wanted to do the right thing with my life, I was simply powerless when it came to controlling my sexuality. It was a constant battle, and although I tried my best to do the right thing, it seemed inevitable that in a short matter of time I would fail, and the cycle of failure I was trapped in would repeat.

My sexual weakness contributed to a promiscuous lifestyle that resulted in a series of relationships involving fornication. I was a fornicator. I went to

Bible college to prepare for ministry and was even elected student body president my senior year. Over one thousand other students chose me as their student leader. I was seen as the kind of individual with an exemplary life that others should emulate and follow. What no one knew was that while I held this public position, I committed sexual sin that would have shocked my peers and ended my administration in disgrace. I lived a double life. I represented myself as one person on the outside, while I struggled secretly with my own personal demons. I was duplicitous, and I was a hypocrite. After graduating from Bible college, I started a ministry, and in a short matter of time became sexually involved with a series of several different girls in the ministry. I was a sexual abuser. It didn't take long for my sin to become common knowledge, and I lost my ministry in public disgrace and humiliation. I was a failure. I married my wife shortly thereafter, and our marriage became an instant disaster. There was a terribly wrong kind of sexual energy alive inside of me, and as I moved toward my wife sexually, the kind of man I was, coupled with my wife's own tragic background, made it almost impossible for her to respond to me emotionally or physically. This led to a kind of relational distance between us that seemed bigger than the Grand Canyon, and I responded horribly over a period of years by acting out in many different ways. I masturbated frequently. I flirted with other women. My heart was filled with lust and my thirsty eyes frequently drank deeply when I noticed a beautiful woman. I visited strip clubs on several occasions, became involved in an emotional affair with one woman, had a one-night stand with another woman, and eventually became involved in an ongoing affair with a close friend's wife. I was a betrayer. I was disloyal and deceitful. I was treacherous and unfaithful. I was a liar. I was an adulterer.

In the end, my life was a complete and total disaster. Mind you, to those on the outside it looked like my life was a success. I had started a remodeling business and built it into a company with over $5,000,000.00 in annual sales. I had over 50 employees. I had a beautiful wife, healthy children, a beautiful house, fancy cars, commercial real estate, financial investments, and money in the bank. But in reality my life was a miserable failure. I was good at accomplishing everything in life that didn't really matter, and lousy at accomplishing what really did matter. More than anything else I wanted a good marriage, but I was completely incapable of making my marriage what I wanted it to be. Eventually, I despaired of life itself. I was so miserable and exhausted. I was so ashamed of the things I had done and the person I had become. I thought to myself, "If this is life, I'm not sure I want it anymore." I knew I couldn't end my own life because I didn't want my kids to live with the fact that their father had committed suicide, so instead I prayed that God would kill me. I was at rock bottom, and at the very center of the disaster was my wounded sexuality. God was not getting much glory from my life, and I think it's fair to say Satan was bringing to bear maximum destruction.

Chains of Bondage

I was in a very real bondage, and my inability to properly control my sexuality was ruining my life. It's as if my life was a tree, and no matter how hard I tried not to allow it, the tree continued to bear the fruit of sexual sin. Although I could keep myself in check through the power of self-effort for short periods of time, ranging from weeks to even months, I would inevitably fail and the fruit of sexual sin would manifest itself again. My attempts to control myself seemed as successful as a dog deciding to never bark again, a goose deciding never to fly south again, or an apple tree deciding not to bear any more apples. Despite my most sincere commitments, there was something alive inside me, something much stronger than the power of my own will, that could rise up spontaneously apart from me and compel my obedience (Romans 7:14-21). It would not be until years later, through a profoundly difficult process of repentance that God required me to work through — and a process I am still in fact walking in — that I would begin to slowly comprehend the nature of my bondage. My bondage consisted of several different "chains" that imprisoned my soul — chains that would eventually be broken off my life one by one as my sexuality and my life were set free by the power of God. These "chains" included, among others, the power of pornography, the influence of older male role models who wrongly taught me what it means to be a man, situations of sexual abuse that had been perpetrated against me, the power of generational sin, and the power of my own sinful flesh. Although these chains were physically invisible, their consequences in my life were very evident. My life was in serious trouble and I desperately needed a savior.

The Bondage Breaker

After reading the preceding brief overview of my life, you can begin to understand what I mean when I say the enemy literally tried to destroy everything of significance in my life through my wounded sexuality. I was in a kind of invisible prison with invisible chains binding my soul. I was a slave. I was lost, in darkness, and completely and utterly incapable of rescuing myself. That's the bad news. But, hold on to your seat, because there's also good news! The good news is that there is Someone who has the power to do for us what we could never do for ourselves. He is the Bondage Breaker! He can cut through bars of steel and gates of bronze (Isaiah 45:2-3). He can shatter invisible chains and open prison doors. He is the Savior, and His name is Jesus! In what I have come to see as one of the most central passages in the entire Bible — the passage Jesus Himself spoke when He started His public ministry — we find a description of the very purpose and ministry of the Savior.

> The Spirit of the Sovereign LORD is on me, because the LORD has anointed me to preach good news to the poor. He has sent me to bind up the brokenhearted, to proclaim freedom for the captives and release from darkness for the prisoners, to proclaim the year of the LORD'S favor and the day of vengeance of our God, to comfort all who mourn, and provide for those who grieve in Zion — to bestow a crown of beauty instead of ashes, the oil of gladness instead of mourning, and a garment of praise instead of a spirit of despair. Isaiah 60:1-3

Jesus did not come to help those who have it all together. He is not just a moral guide or a spiritual cheerleader who encourages us to try real hard and to do our very best. He is not just an example for us to follow. He is the Great Physician, and He didn't come to heal people who think they are healthy and don't need a doctor. He came to heal people who know they are sick. He came to help people who are desperate. He is anointed to preach to the poor. He binds up those who are brokenhearted and in captivity. He brings release for those who are in prison, and comforts those who mourn. He provides for those who grieve and bestows upon them a crown of beauty where there have been ashes, the oil of gladness where there has been mourning, and a garment of praise where there has been despair. And these things are exactly what He has done for me! Glory to God!

Jesus, my Savior and my Redeemer, has totally and radically interrupted and changed my life! He saved me! He rescued me! He redeemed me! He saved my marriage! He changed my heart! He changed my sexuality, and through His power He is enabling me to do something I was unable to do for almost 40 years of my life — 40 years! He is helping me, by His grace, to honor God and my wife with my sexuality! Can you believe it? He's allowing me to glorify Him in the very area of my life that was so wounded and broken, where I had dishonored God for so long. I am now bringing maximum glory to God in the very area of my life the enemy used in his attempt to literally destroy me. God's promise in the Bible is really true. I know because He has kept His promise to me. He has bound up my broken heart and delivered me from the captivity of my prison. He has comforted me and provided for me. He has replaced my ashes with a crown of beauty, my mourning with the oil of gladness, and my despair with a garment of praise. Glory to God forevermore!

And I promise He can do the same for you! That's the purpose of this book: to introduce you to the Bondage Breaker, so He can unleash His redemptive ministry and promise in your life. He can do for you what He has done for me. He can shatter the chains that hold you, change your heart and life, and empower you to bring great glory to God through the very area of your life where you have struggled for so long: your sexuality. Imagine it! Imagine honoring God from the center of your masculinity. Imagine God being pleased with your sexuality, your thought life, what you touch, what you look at, how you use your penis, and how you relate to your wife. As you align your sexuality with God, you will bring maximum glory to Him, the angels in heaven will rejoice, and your life will bring maximum insult to the kingdom of darkness.

An Important Question

Maybe your personal struggle with your sexuality has been nowhere near as intense as mine has been, but regardless of where you stand in this important area of your life, I trust you recognize there is always room for improvement. I picture in my mind's eye a kind of sexual scale from one to ten. Every man falls somewhere along the scale. Number one represents the most perverted, abusive, sick, and twisted sexual deviant you can imagine. It might be someone who stalks, abuses, rapes, and murders children and women. Number ten is the most holy man you can imagine. He honors God completely with his life and sexuality. He virtually never struggles with his thoughts, his eyes, or his actions. My suspicion is that most of us as Christian men do not live at either end of this imaginary scale. Most of us probably live somewhere in the middle of the scale, tending to slide up and down several notches depending on the kind of day or week we are having, or the current state of our relationship with our wife or significant other. My invitation to you as you read this book is to consider the following primary question:

What would it mean for you to honor God in a greater way through the expression of your sexuality?

If you are currently at number five on the previously mentioned scale, what would it mean for you to move to number six? If you are currently at number seven, what would it mean for you to move to number eight? What do you think God would ask of you if He were to ask you to honor Him in a greater way through the expression of your sexuality? Would He ask you to get rid of your pornography? Would He ask you to stop an emotional or sexual affair? Would He ask you to stop masturbating? Would He ask you to have less sex with your wife; or to have more sex with your wife? Would He ask you to behave differently with your eyes or your hands? What would God ask of you? That's the purpose and challenge of this book: to encourage and strengthen you by the grace and power of God to move toward higher levels of sexual purity and freedom in your life, thus empowering you to bring maximum glory to God through your sexuality.

In the pages ahead we will consider the primary "chains" that continue to hold many good men in places of sexual bondage. We will discover how to unleash the redemptive power of the Bondage Breaker in our lives to shatter those chains once and for all. In the meantime, if we are called to honor God with our sexuality, it seems reasonable that we must clearly understand God's expectations regarding our sexuality.

CHAPTER 2

God's Standard of Sexual Purity

The Ultimate Sex Manual...the Bible!

The Bible has a lot to say about sex! Of course, I don't think that should really surprise us, since God is the one who designed the awesome concept of sex! If He had the idea originally, and then designed the male and female bodies accordingly — with hormones, cycles, urges, and desires; with the amazing and perfect ability to copulate and reproduce; and with all the nerve endings in just the right places to maximize the feelings and sensations of physical touch, closeness, and intimacy — it's obvious that He knows best how to use and enjoy such a wonderful gift. After all, He gave this amazing gift to mankind, introduced the first man and woman to each other in a garden while both were completely naked, and then told them to be fruitful and to fill the earth. God really does have a lot to say about sex, but what exactly does He expect from us? Does He really expect us to honor Him from the depth of our sexuality? What in our hearts and lives needs to change in order for God to be well pleased with our lives and to one day say to us, "Well done thy good and faithful servant" (Matthew 25:21)? If we ever hope to reach God's sexual standard for our lives, we need to have a very clear understanding of that standard, and that's the purpose of this chapter.

As you consider the scriptures we are about to look at, it will become increasingly clear that God is deeply concerned about the sexual area of our lives, and He very clearly states His standards in His Word. Although we could study many more passages of scripture concerning sex than the few

19

considered here, for our purposes we will focus on 12 scriptures. For each scripture, we'll make a corresponding observation concerning God's standard of sexual purity for our lives.

SCRIPTURE #1

You shall not commit adultery. Exodus 20:14

On Mount Sinai, in an awesome display of glory and power that included thunder, lightning, thick smoke, and fire, God Himself wrote the Ten Commandments on tablets of stone. In these Commandments, God reduced the entire Bible, including all the Law and all the prophets, into ten concise commands designed to govern man's relationship with not only God, but also his fellow man. In the seventh Commandment, God said, "You shall not commit adultery" (Exodus 20:14). Apparently the issue of human sexuality was of such supreme significance to God that He went out of His way to include it in His most basic list of directives. From this simple scripture we learn something of God's standard of sexuality for our lives...

OBSERVATION #1

The sexual purity of man has always been of central importance to God.

SCRIPTURE #2

The LORD said to Moses, "Speak to the Israelites and say to them; 'I am the LORD your God. You must not do as they do in Egypt, where you used to live, and you must not do as they do in the land of Canaan, where I am bringing you. Do not follow their practices. You must obey my laws and be careful to follow my decrees. I am the LORD your God... Do not have sexual relations with...'" Leviticus 18:1-4, 8

God commands me not to have sex with...

Virtually all of Leviticus 18 talks about sexual relations, and God very clearly reveals further directives for our sexuality by specifically mentioning 16 different ways He does not want us to have sex. Among these prohibitions we are told we should not have sex with our mother, our stepmother, our sister, our stepsister, our granddaughter, our aunt by blood, or our aunt by marriage. We're told not to have sex with our daughter-in-law or our sister-in-law. We're told not to have sex with a woman and then with her daughter or any of her granddaughters. We're told not to have sex with a woman during her monthly menstrual cycle, or with our neighbor's wife. We're told not to have sex with another man, or with animals. At the end of the chapter, God goes on to say that these are detestable practices, that the people who participated in such behavior had become defiled in His sight, and that God punished them accordingly by judging them and vomiting them out of their land. God then warns His children not to follow any of these detestable customs or they too will be judged accordingly. Apparently God has very specific ideas about who we should and should not have sexual relations with. From this passage we learn something more of God's standard of purity for our sexuality...

Observation #2

There are many specific ways God does not want me to express my sexuality.

Scripture #3

If a man commits adultery with another man's wife — with the wife of his neighbor — both the adulterer and the adulteress must be put to death. Leviticus 20:10

God says I must be put to death if I have sex with...

In Leviticus 20 we see the sobering and shocking consequences God required of His people concerning sexual sin. In this alarming passage, God specifically mentions six sexual situations where He actually required the death of the offending persons! These situations include if a man commits adultery with his neighbor's wife; if a man sleeps with his stepmother or daughter-in-law; if a man lies with another man; if a man sleeps with both a woman and her mother; or if a man has sex with an animal.

We see this teaching from the Law, requiring the death of sexual offenders, reflected in John 8:1-11 when the Pharisees wanted to stone a woman who was caught in the act of adultery. "Teacher, this woman was caught in the act of adultery. In the Law Moses commanded us to stone such women. Now what do you say?" Rather than condemning the woman according to the Law, Jesus extended forgiveness to her on the basis of grace — thus giving us hope. Nevertheless, from the alarming passage of Leviticus 20, we see that sexual sin is apparently very serious business to God. In fact, in verses 22-23 of this same passage, God goes on to say that these practices caused Him to "abhor" the people who committed them. The word "abhor" is a significant word that gives us additional insight into God's reaction to sexual sin. According to *Strong's Concordance*, the word means "to be disgusted or anxious, to be distressed or grieved, to loathe, to be vexed and weary." It is a very powerful word and further carries with it the idea of severing oneself or cutting oneself off from the offending party. Evidently sexual sin literally makes God sick to His stomach! From this surprising passage, we learn something more of God's standard for sexual purity...

OBSERVATION #3

The matter of sexual sin is very serious to God and carries with it profoundly severe consequences.

SCRIPTURE #4

You have heard that it was said, 'Do not commit adultery.' But I tell you that anyone who looks at a woman lustfully has already committed adultery with her in his heart. Matthew 5:27-28

In the Sermon on the Mount, Jesus elevates God's standard of sexual purity from the "outside" of our lives to the "inside." He teaches that if we look with lust upon a woman, we have committed adultery with her in our hearts, and we are just as guilty as if we literally physically committed adultery with her. Wow! In Jesus' day, the religious Pharisees were overly concerned with outward righteousness, but Jesus' teaching revealed that God is primarily concerned with the stature of our hearts. In the book of James it is written, "Wash your hands, you sinners, and purify your hearts, you double minded" (James 4:2). "Washing your hands" refers to cleaning up the outside of our lives — what we do, where we go, what we touch, or what we look at — while "purify your hearts" refers to cleaning up the inside of our lives — what we think about and the passionate energy and desires that live within our hearts. With this surprising teaching, Jesus reveals something more to us concerning God's standard of sexual purity for our lives…

OBSERVATION #4

God requires me to be sexually pure on the "inside," including my heart and my mind.

SCRIPTURE #5

Flee from sexual immorality. All other sins a man commits are outside his body, but he who sins sexually sins against his own body. I Corinthians 6:18

According to *Strong's Concordance*, the Greek word translated "flee" in this verse literally means "to run away, to shun, to vanish, escape, and flee away." This is exactly what Joseph did in Genesis 39 when Potiphar's wife attempted to seduce him, and it's exactly what God expects us to do. God did not tell us to *hang around* sexual immorality. He did not tell us to *be careful* with it, or even to *walk away* from it. He told us to **FLEE!** If your life has been anything like mine, I'm sure you can think of several situations where you did not obey this command, and as a result you ended up doing the wrong thing. To me this scripture reveals the practicality of the Word of God. It's as if God knows the weak and sinful tendency of our flesh, and in His wisdom admonishes us to flee from sexual immorality as quickly as possible. God is smart, and He knows that if we put our hand on a hot stove we will get burned, so He warns us to stay away from the stove to begin with. From this biblical command, we learn something more of God's standard for sexual purity...

OBSERVATION #5

God expects me to flee from sexual immorality.

SCRIPTURE #6

Do you not know that your body is a temple of the Holy Spirit, who is in you, whom you have received from God? You are not your own; you were bought at a price. Therefore honor God with your body. I Corinthians 6:19-20

The Bible teaches that at the moment of salvation, the Holy Spirit inhabits our physical body. Our body is therefore the very temple of the Holy Spirit, and we no longer belong to ourselves. We were bought with a price, which was the blood of Jesus, and we are now called to honor God with our physical bodies. In Romans 12:1 we are told to offer our bodies as living sacrifices that are holy and pleasing to God. As Christians we should see our physical body as a kind of possession we have been entrusted with; God gives it to us as a kind of stewardship, a possession He expects us to be faithful with, and a possession we will one day give an account for. In the same way

I may have a car, a house, a farm, or a computer, I also have a physical body, and since God expects me to honor Him with everything He has entrusted me with, this includes my physical body. I think we have a dangerous tendency to gain our identity from our body, when in reality we should see it as a possession God has entrusted to us and with which we are called to honor Him. I believe that's what this scripture is talking about. From this scripture, we learn something more of God's standard of sexual purity for our lives...

Observation #6

I am called to honor God with my physical body.

Scripture #7

Do you not know that in a race all the runners run, but only one gets the prize? Run in such a way as to get the prize. Everyone who competes in the games goes into strict training. They do it to get a crown that will not last; but we do it to get a crown that will last forever. Therefore I do not run like a man running aimlessly; I do not fight like a man beating the air. No, I beat my body and make it my slave so that after I have preached to others, I myself will not be disqualified for the prize. I Corinthians 9:24-27

With this beautiful metaphor, the Apostle Paul reminds us that the runners in a championship race go into "strict training" as they prepare their bodies for maximum performance and competition. Paul tells us that while they do all this work to achieve a crown that will not last, that we are competing for a crown that will last forever. He goes on to encourage us to "beat" our bodies and make them our "slave" so we will not be disqualified for the prize. According to *Strong's Concordance*, the Greek word translated "beat" literally means "to hit under the eye, to buffet or disable like a boxer would his opponent." The word translated "slave" means "to be a slave driver, to subdue and bring into subjection." It's a very graphic image of a person fighting, in a sense, his very own body as he strives for excellence and maximum performance in a race. It almost seems that the athlete is really facing two opponents: one is, of course, the other competitor, but the other is his very own physical body. It's implied that before the runner can beat the other contestants in the race on the outside, he has to first conquer the greater opponent of his own body on the inside. Eventually it's the runner against others, but first it's the runner against himself. Only one runner will get the prize, and if we are to attain the crown God has set before each one of our lives, we must employ strict discipline and mastery of our own bodies. Only then will we compete well and finish strong. From this scripture, we learn something more of God's standard of sexual purity for our lives…

OBSERVATION #7

I am expected to master my physical body. I should be in control of it, and it should not be in control of me.

SCRIPTURE #8

I have written you in my letter not to associate with sexually immoral people — not at all meaning the people of this world who are immoral, or the greedy and swindlers, or idolaters. In that case you would have to leave this world. But now I am writing you that you must not associate with anyone who calls himself a brother but is sexually immoral or greedy, an idolater or a slanderer, a drunkard or a swindler. With such a man do not even eat… Expel the wicked man from among you. I Corinthians 5:9-13

In this surprising passage, Paul is rebuking the Church at Corinth for tolerating sexual immorality among the believers. In this situation a man in the church was having sex with his stepmother. In verse 2 Paul says the church should have been filled with grief and put out of the fellowship the man who committed this sin. Apparently Paul saw sexual sin as so completely unacceptable that he believed people should actually be placed under church discipline because of it! This high standard makes me wonder what our churches might look like if we removed all those who are guilty of sexual sin.

Hmmm... From this scripture, we learn something more of God's standard of sexual purity for our lives...

Observation #8

Sexual sin is so seriously unacceptable it
warrants church discipline.

Scripture #9

It is God's will that you should be sanctified: that you should avoid sexual immorality; that each of you should learn to control his own body in a way that is holy and honorable, not in passionate lust like the heathen, who do not know God; and that in this matter no one should wrong his brother or take advantage of him. The Lord will punish men for all such sins, as we have already told you and warned you. For God did not call us to be impure, but to live a holy life. Therefore, he who rejects this instruction does not reject man but God, who gives you his Holy Spirit. I Thessalonians 4:3-8

According to *Strong's Concordance*, the Greek word translated "sanctified" in this passage literally means "purity." Paul is point-blank telling us that it is God's will for our lives to be pure. He then defines what he means by purity in the very context of the same passage by saying we should avoid sexual immorality and control our bodies in a way that is holy and honorable to God. In Titus 2:14 we are told that "our great God and Savior, Jesus Christ, gave himself for us to redeem us from all wickedness and to purify for himself a people of his very own." Wow! We're told in this scripture that the reason Jesus gave His life for us was to *purify* for Himself a people of His very own. Apparently the purity of His people is of incredible significance to God. In Ephesians 5:25-27 we are told that,

Christ loved the church and gave himself up for her to make her holy, cleansing her by the washing with water through the word, and to present her to himself as a radiant church, without stain or wrinkle or any other blemish, but holy and blameless.

I don't know if you got the full impact of this scripture, but it is incredibly powerful! (In fact, I highly recommend that you stop reading for a few minutes, take the time to meditate on this scripture, and let it dawn on you what is really being said here.) Paul is using the beautiful imagery of a wedding. In the image, Christ is the groom and the Church is the bride. We're told that Christ loved the Church and gave Himself up for her in order to cleanse her through a kind of washing. According to *Strong's Concordance*, in the original language the word "cleanse" means "to make clean, to purge, or to purify." The word "wash" means "to give the whole person a bath or a washing." It's really an awesome word because of the three possible words Paul could have used here, he used the word that conveys the most complete picture of cleansing. One word Paul could have used means to wash clothes. Another word he could have used means to wash only a part of the body. The final word, and the one Paul chose to use in this passage to describe the way Christ *washes* his bride, is to bathe the entire person! In other words, Christ doesn't just want a bride with clean clothes, or a bride that is partially clean. He wants a bride who has been completely bathed — the entire person — and made clean. Awesome!

This same thought is further reinforced as Paul continues that Christ will one day present to Himself "a radiant church, without stain or wrinkle or any other blemish, but holy and blameless." If you want to do a splendid study that will speak into your heart, take your concordance and look up the meaning of this verse's six key words: *radiant, stain, wrinkle, blemish, holy, blameless*. These words paint a wonderful picture of the kind of bride Jesus wants, and the kind of bride Jesus died to cleanse! Because of limited space, I will comment for our purpose on only one of these words. According to *Strong's Concordance*, the word "wrinkle" in this passage means "a fold, as drawing together, a wrinkle, especially on the face." When I discovered this meaning, it blessed my heart deeply and confirmed again what I knew the Lord was trying to show me. When I first read the passage I assumed the words *stain, wrinkle*, and *blemish* referred to the bride's dress. Surely, I reasoned, a groom would want his bride, as she appears at the end of the aisle and begins to walk toward him, to be adorned in a beautiful, spotless, ironed, and wrinkle-free dress. But in reality that is not at all what Jesus wants from His bride. As mentioned, the word "wrinkle" literally means "a wrinkle especially on the face." In other words, Jesus cares more about His bride than He does about what she is wearing. He prepares His bride for the coming wedding celebration by washing her and removing the wrinkles, not from her dress, but from her face! His ultimate goal is to prepare His bride; to wash her and cleanse her; to remove every stain, wrinkle, and blemish from her; so He can one day receive her as a holy, blameless, and glorious bride. Glory be to God! Based upon this scripture, we learn something more of God's standard of sexual purity for our lives...

OBSERVATION #9

Purity is God's will for my life.

SCRIPTURE #10

For this reason a man will leave his father and mother and be united to his wife, and the two will become one flesh. This is a profound mystery — but I am talking about Christ and the church. Ephesians 5:31-32

In this beautiful scripture, we learn that the "one flesh" union of a man and his wife illustrates the profound mystery of Christ and the Church. According to *Strong's Concordance*, the Greek word translated "united" in this verse literally means "to glue together." It's a picture of unity. It's a picture of oneness that can never be broken. Imagine taking two pieces of wood and gluing them together. They would no longer be two separate pieces of wood, but they would instead be one new piece. Just as nothing can ever separate Christ from His bride, the Church, God intends that nothing should ever separate a man and a woman once they are married.

This picture is significant in its implications. It teaches us that it is God's intention that a man becomes "one flesh" with his wife. It is God's design from the beginning that each man finds one woman whom he will "unite" with, or that he will be "glued" to. She, of all women, is to be his center of attention. She is to be his focus. She is to be his all and all. She is to be the object of his delight, desire, and passion. God did not say he should be unit-

ed to many different women. He said a man should be "glued" to one
woman: his wife.

This truth and God's intention from the beginning is further illustrated,
I believe, by the act of creation itself. After God created Adam, He created
all the animals and allowed Adam to name them. Upon completion of this
task, Adam noticed that although each of the animals had a corresponding
mate, he himself did not have a "suitable helper." In response to Adam's
need, God caused him to fall into a deep sleep, and while he was sleeping
the Lord took one of his ribs and made a woman for Adam. The Bible says
that when God presented the woman to Adam, He said, "This is now bone
of my bones and flesh of my flesh; she shall be called woman, for she was
taken out of man. For this reason a man will leave his father and mother and
be united to his wife, and they will become one flesh" (Genesis 2:23-24).

What was God's solution to Adam's dilemma? What was God's solution
to Adam's aloneness? What was God's solution to Adam's need? God created
one woman and gave her to Adam! God intended that in this provision, in
this one woman, Adam would find the answers — relationally, emotionally,
physically, sexually — to everything he would ever need as a man. God did
not create several women and bring them to Adam. He created one, and so
we conclude that it is in the confines of our relationship with the one
woman God has given us that we can find the answer to every need we could
ever know as men. Because of God's provision for us in our one woman, we
never have to look anywhere else for the satisfaction or completion of our
lives. She is to complete us! She is to be our friend and our lover! She is to
be the only object of our desire, passion, and attention! We are to be "glued"
to her, and to be one flesh with her. She is God's provision for our lives, and
we should never look anywhere else but to her for the fulfillment and completion of our relational needs as men.

Of course the woman was never intended to replace God Himself in
Adam's life. Adam was still to know, love, walk with, and serve God. But the
fact remains that God Himself said, "It is not good for the man to be alone.
I will make a helper suitable for him" (Genesis 2:18). It's as if God recognized that Adam had an *aloneness* about his life that even God Himself could
not complete, and as a result God provided the one woman Adam needed.
From these amazing scriptures, we learn something more of God's standard
of sexual purity for our lives...

Observation # 10

It is God's will that I have a "one flesh" union
with my wife, and that she be the sole object of
my desire and attention.

Scripture # 11

Since there is so much immorality, each man should have his
own wife, and each woman her own husband. The husband
should fulfill his marital duty to his wife, and likewise the
wife to her husband. The wife's body does not belong to her
alone but also to her husband. In the same way, the
husband's body does not belong to him alone but also to his
wife. Do not deprive each other except by mutual consent
and for a time, so that you may devote yourselves to prayer.
Then come together again so that Satan will not tempt you
because of your lack of self-control. I Corinthians 7:2-5

In this passage, Paul teaches that the solution to immorality should be found
in your marital partner alone. He warns that wives and husbands should be
careful to fulfill one another's needs through one another's bodies. He warns
further that we should not deprive one another unless it is by mutual consent, and then only for a period of time, so we will not be tempted beyond
our level of self-control. Paul is acknowledging that if too much time passes
without marital sexual expression that we risk being tempted by the enemy
due to our lack of self-control. It's as if Paul is saying, "If it's been a while
since you have had sex, and you begin to feel tempted by the enemy toward
anything immoral, and if you are beginning to struggle with sexual self-control, GO TO YOUR WIFE!" Paul is clearly teaching that the sole object of
your sexual desire, attention, and expression should be your wife. He does
not leave room for any other type of sexual expression or fulfillment. Paul
does not say we should masturbate to relieve ourselves and avoid further
temptation. He does not say we should look at pornography or go to anoth-

er woman to relieve ourselves. The only solution he provides to avoid ongoing temptation or in the event of faltering self-control is our wives. Your wife is a God-given gift, and you are to find in her alone the fulfillment of your sexual needs and expression. From this scripture, we learn something more of God's standard of sexual purity for our lives…

OBSERVATION # 11

It is God's will that my wife alone be the object
of my sexual fulfillment.

WARNING!

Be careful how you interpret the previous scripture from I Corinthians! I believe many men, including myself, have used this passage to justify the presence of immorality in their lives with thoughts like, "My wife doesn't believe these verses! She does not allow me to have access to her body the way the Bible says! That's the real source of my problem! If my wife would only have more sex with me and let me do the things I want to do, I wouldn't be so tempted to look at other women, to masturbate, and all that! It's really my wife's fault! I should not be held so responsible for what I do wrong, because if she was keeping up her end of the bargain, I wouldn't have such a problem with my sexuality!" Come on now guys! Have you ever had these kinds of thoughts or feelings?

In my particular case, I literally fought with God for about 15 years because of these verses! I knew I had a right to my wife's body, but she refused to give me access — partially because of her own issues related to the deep wounds of her past, and partially because of the wrongness that lived in me and the violations of relationship I had perpetrated against her. As a result of her inability to respond to me emotionally and sexually, I raged against her and God, and used her behavior as an excuse to justify my own sin. It was eventually through the long and difficult process of repentance God required of me that I slowly began to recognize I was still responsible for the purity of my own heart, mind, and life — regardless of my wife's actions or decisions.

It was during this difficult process, while my wife and I were not having any kind of sexual relations, that God brought me to the place of a vow where He required me to surrender my sexuality, my body, and my penis to Him in a deeper way than I ever had before. God apparently wanted to do a deep work in my heart first, and as I learned to cooperate with Him, and as He slowly began to change my heart and life, He was then able to go to work on my wife and slowly begin changing her into the woman He was calling her to be. If you and your wife are not finding sexual fulfillment in one another — and if your marriage is so bad you don't see how God's standard can ever become a reality — DON'T GIVE UP HOPE! I promise that if you first do your part by repenting and allowing God to work deeply in your heart, life, and sexuality, that He is big enough to handle your wife, save your marriage, and let you find in your wife the fulfillment of all your sexual needs.

SCRIPTURE #12

But among you there must not be even a hint of sexual immorality, or of any kind of impurity, or of greed, because these are improper for God's holy people. Ephesians 5:3

Based upon this scripture, we learn that God does NOT grade on a curve. Paul clearly says that there should not be even a "hint" of sexual immorality, or any kind of impurity in our lives. But we have a way of watering down God's standard, don't we? We can rationalize, justify, explain, and "yeah, but" with the best of them! For example:

- Yeah, but you don't understand! My wife won't have sex with me!
- Yeah, but you don't understand! This woman at work is driving me crazy and I figure it's better to masturbate than to have an affair!
- Yeah, but you don't understand! It's not that big a deal if I just look at those girls in the bikinis. After all, I can't help it if God made me a man and gave me all these hormones!
- Yeah, but you don't understand! Almost every man looks at dirty magazines, and I can't help it if they're at work every day!
- Yeah, but you don't understand! If only my wife was not so _____, (fill in the blank — fat, stupid, sloppy, sensitive, demanding, prideful, selfish, etc.) then I would find her more attractive. I have to get my kicks somewhere, don't I?

Sorry guys! I don't see fine print in the Bible where God gave "exceptions" to His rules. He didn't say, "There should not be a hint of sexual immorality among you, unless _____ (fill in the blank with your excuse). Then in this case it's understandable if there is sexual immorality." No such luck! He simply said, "… not even a hint of sexual immorality…" I will neither apologize for God's standard of sexual purity nor water it down to make our lives easier! God's Word says what it says, and God means what He says. When God went to work on my life, He didn't really go easy on me. He required me to stand up and face the reality of who and what He was calling me to be as a man, and I believe He's asking the same of many other men at this time. It's time we get serious about honoring God with our lives…and our sexuality! From this scripture, we learn something more of God's standard of sexuality for our lives…

OBSERVATION #12

There should not be even a hint of impurity in my life.

A Quick Review

As we conclude this chapter, let's review the twelve observations we have made concerning God's standard of sexual purity for our lives.

1. The sexual purity of man has always been of central importance to God.
2. There are many specific ways God does not want me to express my sexuality.
3. The matter of sexual sin is very serious to God and carries with it profoundly severe consequences.
4. God requires me to be sexually pure on the "inside," including my heart and my mind.
5. God expects me to flee from sexual immorality.
6. I am called to honor God with my physical body.
7. I am expected to master my physical body. I should be in control of it, and it should not be in control of me.
8. Sexual sin is so seriously unacceptable it warrants church discipline.

9. Purity is God's will for my life.
10. It is God's will that I have a "one flesh" union with my wife, and that she be the sole object of my desire and attention.
11. It is God's will that my wife alone be the object of my sexual fulfillment.
12. There should not be even a hint of impurity in my life.

As indicated at the beginning of this chapter, I do not believe these 12 observations are a complete representation of God's standard of sexual purity for our lives, but they are a good foundation. We could study many more passages of scripture and continue to refine our understanding of God's holy standards. However, as we reflect upon these 12 standards from God's Word, we should realize maybe clearer than ever exactly what God is asking of us from the sexual area of our lives.

A Working Definition

As God worked deeply in my life to redeem my wounded sexuality, He eventually brought me to the place where He challenged me through the voice of a Christian friend to make my wife the sole object of my sexual desire and expression. That meant that I could no longer derive any sexual pleasure in any way from anything or anyone but my wife. Once I established that standard in my life, any "fuzzy" or "questionable" areas were virtually eliminated and it was clear what was unacceptable behavior in my quest to honor both God and my wife through my sexuality. I clearly knew from that point forward what I should be doing with every part of my life in relation to my sexuality, including my mind, eyes, hands, touch, words, penis, and any other aspect of my life. Once I held that standard — my wife being the sole object of my sexual desire and expression — I could easily measure any situation against the standard and quickly determine my corresponding behavior. For example:

- If I saw a beautiful woman and caught myself looking at her inappropriately, I immediately knew I should look away.
- If I came across a dirty magazine somewhere and was tempted to look at the colorful pictures, I immediately knew I should turn away.
- If I was in a social setting and felt a "vibe" from another woman as she began to flirt with me, I immediately knew I should not reciprocate.

- If I was tempted to masturbate because I had a hard day, because I was depressed, or because I knew it would help me fall asleep faster, I immediately knew I could not participate in such behavior.
- If I somehow found myself daydreaming about an old girlfriend, or fantasizing about having sex with another woman, or reliving a wrong sexual encounter in my mind, I immediately knew I had to turn those thoughts off and push them away.

That's how God worked in my life. As I followed Him through the difficult process of repentance He required of me, He slowly began to heal and redeem my broken sexuality and transform my heart and life so I was empowered by His grace to fulfill the new standard He had revealed to me. For this reason, for me as a married man, my working definition of sexual purity became...

My wife is the sole object of my sexual desire and expression!

CHAPTER 3

REPENTANCE

A Desperate Dilemma

Imagine you are sailing across the ocean on a luxury ocean liner. One evening while you are standing near the guardrail, and no one else is around to see you, you somehow slip and fall overboard. Your heart is gripped with fear and panic as your body plunges deep into the dark, ice-cold water, and you struggle with all your strength back toward the surface where you gasp for precious air. You immediately begin to scream for help with all your might, but you watch in horror as the dull roar of the ship's engines continue to propel it past you, leaving you in the shadowy water of its churning wake.

You continue to scream in desperation, but quickly realize the futility of your effort as the ship moves away from you at a surprising rate of speed. Everything on the outside suddenly begins moving in a weird kind of slow motion as your mind races in a panic in its vain attempt to find a solution to your unexpected dilemma. Oddly, it occurs to you that the ship seems to be moving a lot faster as you watch it from the water than it seemed to be moving when you were on it. You struggle to keep your head above the chilly water as you dog-paddle with your remaining strength, and your body rises and falls as each swell of water passes beneath you. With a growing sense of hopelessness you realize the desperation of your situation. You have fallen overboard. The water is ice cold. You are in the dark. No one knows you are gone. You do not have a life jacket. You are hundreds of miles from the closest land. You are in a desperate dilemma!

A Savior

If you were in this dilemma, do you know what you would need? You would need a savior! You would need someone to do for you what you could never do for yourself. You would be hopelessly lost and desperate. You would be hopelessly incapable of rescuing yourself. No matter how hard you would try; no matter how sincere your effort; no matter your strength; no matter how many swimming lessons you've had; you could not save yourself. You would be doomed. You would be in the middle of a situation that is far bigger and far more powerful than you. You would not be big enough, strong enough, smart enough, or wise enough to work things out on your own. You would be completely lost, and if your own resources were all you had to draw upon, you wouldn't have a chance in the world of making it out alive. You would need a savior, and if a savior failed to come along, then you would not be saved!

Man Overboard

Gentlemen, I propose that you and I are indeed the man described in the above dilemma! While sailing on the ocean liner called "life," we fell into the dark, ice-cold water of our own sexuality. We've been dog-paddling for a long time now. We've been doing our best to keep our heads above the water. We've been trying to do the right thing, but in our hearts we know that we have been far less, and settled for far less, than being the men God is calling us to be. Despite our best efforts to keep our lives together and to honor God with our sexuality, the fact remains that many of us are lower on the "sexual purity scale" than we know we should be, and we're not where God wants us to be. Thankfully almost no one ever broaches the subject of male sexuality in the context of church, so we're able to fly below the "radar" and maintain our "good Christian man" image on the outside as we move about in an incognito fashion in our Christian communities. We easily dismiss our secret struggles — whatever they may be — as we rationalize that every man has struggles. We tell ourselves that God understands, and we're really not that different than most other guys. We know that if the people around us somehow found out about our secret struggles, thoughts, and actions, we would have an overwhelming sense of shame because of such exposure. As a result, we're careful to snuggle ever deeper into the bushes that are hiding our shame, and virtually no one knows who we really are or what we really struggle with; not a friend, not our pastor, not our wife, not even our accountability partner. The fact is we are in a desperate dilemma. We need someone to rescue us! We need someone to do for us what we could never do for ourselves! We need someone who is bigger, stronger, smarter, and wiser than us! We need someone to help us! We need a savior, and if a savior does not come along, we will not be saved!

Warrior Poets or P.O.W.s?

> In the year of our Lord, 1314, patriots of Scotland, starving and outnumbered, charged the fields of Banocburn. They fought like warrior poets. They fought like Scotsmen, and won their freedom.

I love these words from the end of the movie *Braveheart*. The patriots of Scotland, against overwhelming odds, fought like warrior poets and won their freedom. These words inspire me because I believe that we too are called to be warrior poets. We are patriots of God's kingdom, and we are called to fight for freedom; the freedom of our own hearts, the freedom of our wives and children, the freedom of others, and the freedom of our sexuality, among many other things. But there is one thing we better not lose sight of as we bask in the warm thought of being warriors: warriors are called into battle with a very real enemy. In fact, if there were no enemies then there would be no battle, and if there were no battle then there would be no need for warrior poets. As Christian men, we must wake up from the slumber that has clouded our way of thinking and seeing for so long. Life is not just about our comfort. The true purpose of our lives is not to make as much money as we can, drive a nice car, get a bigger house, and lower our golf handicap. Remember? We are called to bring maximum glory to God, and to allow God to unleash through our lives maximum destruction upon the kingdom of darkness. We are called to be warrior poets! That's the purpose of our lives! The spiritual battle we are involved with and called to participate in as warrior poets is not a fairy tale. Satan and his cohorts are not just evil comic book personalities like the Joker from *Batman*, or the Wicked Witch from *The Wizard of Oz*. This is a real battle! There is a real enemy! The stakes are incredibly high! You are a major player, and your active participation and maximum contribution are desperately needed!

What's the point? Well, in the first chapter of this book I shared with you how the enemy literally tried to destroy my life through the primary vehicle of my wounded and misguided sexuality. He did a pretty good job of taking

me out of the battle for many years, and effectively neutralized my contribution to the Kingdom of God because of my continuous struggle with and
resulting consequences of the sexual area of my life. With precision accuracy, the enemy effectively reduced me from the status of warrior poet to
P.O.W., prisoner of war, and my fear is that the enemy is doing the same
thing to many other warrior poets in the Kingdom of God. That's the point!

I'm afraid there are many good men in the Kingdom who are not
engaged on the front lines of battle because they too have been neutralized
by their wounded sexuality. They may go to church, give their money, participate in programs and home groups, and attend men's retreats, among
other things. But the fact is that their personal lives and connections with
God are hollow and powerless. They have been diminished to sitting in the
pew week after week, and they are not rising up in the power of the Holy
Spirit as warrior poets to do the exploits God has designed for their lives,
because their sexual sin has taken them out of the battle. I see in my heart a
vision of churches full of men — a great company of hundreds and thousands of warriors — sitting in their pews and looking very good on the outside. But on the inside, where no one but God can see, they are being held
captive by invisible chains that are anchored to weights like pornography, the
internet, strip clubs, impure thoughts, wandering eyes, masturbation, adultery, perversions, and God knows what else.

Come on, guys! It's time to call a spade a spade. It's time to be honest. It's
time to face the truth. It's time to stop candy-coating, minimizing, justifying,
and rationalizing our sin away. "Surely you desire truth in the inner parts; you
teach me wisdom in the inmost place" (Psalm 51:6). It's time to stop justifying ourselves with the following lies from the pit of hell: *It's alright. It's no big
deal. Every guy struggles with this. You're not really any different than the other
guys in church. They all do stuff like this. Don't worry about it.* The devil has
told us these lies long enough, because it's not alright, and because the average guy in church is not the standard God is going to measure our lives
against. He's going to measure our lives against the standard of His holy
Word, and one day we will give an account for ourselves regardless of what
the other guys at church do or don't do. The previous chapter provided a
small glimpse of the sexual standard God is calling us to, and He is calling us
to purity. He is preparing a radiant bride "without stain or wrinkle or any
other blemish, but holy and blameless" (Ephesians 5:27). That's what He is
asking of us, and I believe it's high time we get serious about our christianity
and get back in the battle as the warrior poets we are called to be.

The Kitchen Sink

One time our kitchen sink was draining very slowly, so my wife asked me to take a look at it. By the way, that was a great act of faith on her behalf, because I am anything but a handyman! I retrieved my tools, climbed under the sink, and went to war with the pipes that were defiantly challenging me. In a short matter of time I had disassembled the trap along with a couple other connecting pipes, and when I looked through them I immediately saw the problem. They were literally almost closed shut because they were filled with horrible, stinky, nasty, junky stuff. The gunk began to stick on the sides of the pipes, and as it got a grip accordingly, it apparently became easier and easier for more junk to pile up. Over time this alien build-up had continued, and the final result was a sink that was incapable of fulfilling its purpose, destiny, and calling in life. Wow!

It was some time later the Holy Spirit reminded me of the kitchen sink and spoke deeply to my heart through the corresponding picture He revealed to me. He showed me that Jesus is the living water that wants to flow through me, that I am like the kitchen sink, and sin is like the horrible, stinky, nasty, junky stuff clogging up the pipes. Do not be deceived! Do not minimize, justify, or rationalize your sin. Do not let the devil talk you into believing that your sin is no big deal. The fact of the matter is that our sin is a very big deal. God is a Holy God. In fact, He is so holy, awesome, and glorious that I don't even have a clue how holy and awesome He really is. I cannot begin to comprehend His holiness, and I cannot begin to use words to convey to you how holy our God is. Sin is very serious business to God, and He does not like, bless, or want to hang around sin. When there is sin in our lives, it deeply grieves the heart of God, hindering His ability to flow in power through us, and thus His ability to bless and use us.

What's the point? The point is we need to clean out our pipes! We need to get serious with God and serious with our sin. We need to get cleaned up so living water can flow through our lives in power, so invisible chains can be broken once and for all, and so we can rise up as warrior poets and perform exploits for God. This will bring maximum glory to God and bring maximum destruction to the kingdom of darkness! Glory to God! I may not know you personally, but I believe you really want more of God in your life. I believe it because you have had the courage to read this far. You are hungry. You want more for your life and your future. You want to be a warrior poet. You want a life of significance for the Kingdom. You want your life to matter. You want to perform exploits for God. You want to clean out your pipes, stop making excuses for your sin, and honor God with sexual purity in your life.

Perfume & Pigs

Let me go ahead and put your mind at ease by telling you now that sexual purity is not about self-effort. The remainder of this book is not going to suggest a process of tips, strategies, steps, or techniques we can follow in order to somehow do better in the sexual area of our lives. The fact is I truly believe we cannot do better. The Bible clearly teaches that we are utterly incapable of saving ourselves from sin in any way. To get saved from the penalty of sin in my life (justification), I had to trust my Savior, Jesus, to do for me what I could never do for myself. I could never take away my own sin, no matter how hard I might try. No matter how many times I might go to church, or how much money I might give, or how many good deeds I might do, or how hard I might try to clean up my life, I could never, ever take away my own sin and make myself acceptable to God (Ephesians 2:8-9). The only way to be delivered from the penalty of my sin would be for Jesus to deliver me, and if Jesus didn't deliver me I would go straight to the pit of hell when I die.

In much the same way, the Bible says in order for me to get saved from the power of sin in my life (sanctification), I have to trust my Savior, Jesus, to do for me what I could never do for myself (Romans 8:1-2). I could never overcome the power of sin in my life; no matter how hard I might try. No matter how many accountability partners I have, or how many tips, techniques, strategies, or steps I try to follow, I could never, ever break the power of sin — including sexual sin — in my life, thus making myself a better Christian. The only way to be delivered from the power of sin in my life would be for Jesus to deliver me, and if Jesus didn't deliver me I would remain forever in the bondages, addictions, sinful patterns, and chains that ensnare me.

For example, a farmer could take a pig out of the barnyard and do his very best to change its life and clean it up. He could bathe and perfume the pig, and tie a yellow ribbon around its neck. But do you know what the pig would do as soon as the farmer released it back into the barnyard? It would run as fast as it could and jump right back in the mud and slop! And friend, that's about the same result any of us will ever get from self-effort, good works, or trying harder. If the only resources we have to draw upon are our own — our own strength, power, wisdom, and ability — we are hopelessly lost! We might try real hard for a while, and we might clean ourselves up on the outside for a while, but in the end we will run and jump right back in the mud and slop, just like the pig.

No, friend, the answer to our desperate dilemma is not more self-effort. There's only one answer to our dilemma, and His name is Jesus! Jesus is our only hope! There is no other way to be set free from sin! There is no other way for me to approach God and to make myself acceptable to Him, except for Jesus! There is no way for me to break the power of sinful habits in my life, or to make myself sexually pure before God. There is only one way, and there is only one name, and that name is Jesus! But guess what? This is really good news because that's exactly what Jesus came to do and wants to do in our lives. Remember? The foundational scripture for this book, and the central passage in the Bible that describes the very reason Jesus came from heaven to earth gives us our only hope.

> The Spirit of the Sovereign LORD is on me, because the LORD has anointed me to preach good news to the poor. He has sent me to bind up the brokenhearted, to proclaim freedom for the captives and release from darkness for the prisoners, to proclaim the year of the LORD'S favor and the day of vengeance of our God, to comfort all who mourn, and provide for those who grieve in Zion — to bestow a crown of beauty instead of ashes, the oil of gladness instead of mourning, and a garment of praise instead of a spirit of despair. Isaiah 60:1-3

Glory to God! The very reason Jesus came was to proclaim freedom for captives and release for prisoners! He came to do for us what we could never do for ourselves. He came to provide for us freedom from the penalty of sin so we could go to heaven when we die, and He came to provide for us freedom from the power of sin so we could walk in victory over sin — including sexual sin — in this life. No, friend! If we are seeking sexual purity, we do not need more self-effort; we need a genuine encounter with Jesus!

Repentance

If it's true that Jesus is the only solution to the problem of sin for both the non-Christian (in order to get saved) and the Christian (in order to be set

free from the power of sin), then it's profoundly significant that we understand the importance of repentance. Why? Because repentance is the stature
of heart that enables us to come to Jesus. Before a non-Christian can come
to Jesus, he has to repent. It is, in fact, the very process of repentance that
enables a person's heart to see his sin, realize his need, and come to Christ by
faith in order to be saved. In the same way, it is the process of repentance
that enables a Christian's heart to see his sin, realize his need, and come to
Christ by faith in order to be delivered. Without Jesus there is no freedom
from sin, and without repentance we are incapable of coming to Jesus for
rescue. Repentance is absolutely essential because without it we are incapable
of realizing our need and moving toward Christ.

Luke 15 depicts the beautiful story of the prodigal son. Early in the story
the son takes his inheritance, moves away from his father, and with his wild
lifestyle squanders everything he has. His life is a picture of autonomy, inde-
pendence, and rebellion. By his attitude and actions he is pretty much giving his father the "finger." He's undoubtedly thinking thoughts like, "You
can take a flying leap, dad! I'm not interested in doing things your way. I'm
not interested in being close to you or spending time with you. I want to be
in charge of my own life and I want to do things my way. Your whole deal
is a little too stuffy and rigid for me, dad. I want to have some fun. I think
I can manage my life just fine without you, so give me my inheritance, and
I'll see you later."

Just like us, after doing things his own rebellious, autonomous way, the
son ends up lost, alone, hungry, and in big trouble. A severe famine comes
into the land, and through a progressive series of downward events, the son
eventually finds himself in the pigpen of life. He realizes in his heart that his
way may not be the best way after all. Despite his very best efforts to manage his life and to make things work, he realizes that he is not big enough,
strong enough, wise enough, or smart enough to manage his own life after
all. He has come to the end of himself, and he is at the precious place of glorious ruin.

As he comes to his senses, the son does the only thing he knows he can
do. He decides to return home to his father. When he does, the most
remarkable and beautiful thing happens. His father, filled with compassion
and joy, runs to him, throws his arms around him, and kisses him. The
father rejoices over the lost son who has returned home, and a grand celebration follows.

Friend, I propose this is exactly what repentance is. Repentance is realizing how desperately we need the Father and returning home to Him. It's realizing that we cannot manage our lives by ourselves, and if left to ourselves we will only make a mess of things. Repentance is coming to the end of ourselves, and the end of our self-effort, and turning back to God. It's the end of self-sufficiency and the beginning of God-sufficiency. Repentance is realizing that our way is not the best way. Repentance is the exact opposite of autonomy and rebellion; it's humility, submission, and dependence. Repentance is finally accepting the fact that even our best effort will never be good enough. It's accepting the fact that if the Father doesn't save us, we will never be saved. Repentance is realizing we are men overboard; that we are totally lost and incapable of saving ourselves. It's crying out from broken hearts of desperation to the Father to do for us what we could never do for ourselves. Repentance is the stature of heart that enables us to move toward Jesus so He can rescue us and unleash the redemptive ministry of Isaiah 61 in our lives.

You are Invited

For many, many years I tried to manage the wrongness of my sexuality my own way, and I ended up in the pigpen. I dog-paddled for a long time, trying to keep my head above the water, but it wasn't until I began moving back toward the Father on a pathway of repentance that my life and my sexuality began to change. Tips and techniques did not rescue me. Trying harder, doing my best, and accountability partners did not rescue me. Jesus is the one who rescued me, and Jesus is the one who will rescue you, too! Therefore, the remainder of this book is not about tips and techniques designed to help you try harder and better manage your sexuality. Instead, the remainder of this book is about repentance, and will invite you into a process of repentance specifically over the sexual area of your life. It is a process designed to draw our hearts toward Jesus through deeper levels of repentance. By God's grace it will help us to see our sin; to see the invisible chains that have been binding us; to realize how incapable we are of rescuing ourselves; and to move toward Jesus — the Bondage Breaker — as our only source of hope and life. Are you ready?

PART 2

Breaking the Roots of Bondage

Fruit & Roots

Fruit is always the result of roots. An apple hangs on a twig. The twig connects to a small branch, which connects to a bigger branch. The bigger branch connects to the tree trunk, which eventually gropes its way into the ground through an intricate root system. The roots absorb moisture and nutrients from the surrounding soil, which nourishes the tree and empowers it to produce more apples. Fruit is always the result of roots.

For a long time I did not clearly understand why I struggled so deeply with my sexuality. I had become a Christian. I would try my very best to do the right thing, and I would pray to God for help. But despite my best effort I seemed hopelessly trapped in a continuous cycle of temptation, defeat, and failure. It wasn't until I was well-along the path of my redemptive healing that I slowly began to understand why I had struggled so deeply for so long: fruit is always the result of roots! My life continued to manifest the fruit of sexual sin because there were sinful roots in my life that had never been properly dealt with, and as a result they continued producing wrong fruit. It really didn't matter how old I happened to be at any given time. I could have been 20, 30, or 40 years old, just like an apple tree growing older with each decade. What mattered was where my roots were planted. Comparing my sexuality to a tree, I began to understand that the sexual roots that had been

47

established very early in my life were wrong and dishonoring to God. No wonder I struggled so deeply for so long. No wonder my life continued to produce the fruit of sexual sin.

As I began to see and understand the roots of my sexuality, I began to understand why the enemy had held me captive for so long. It was only then, as I slowly walked with Jesus on the pathway of repentance, that He graciously began to expose each sinful root and sever it through the power of the Holy Spirit. I was being set free, not through tips and techniques, and not through self-effort, but through the redemptive and powerful Isaiah 61 ministry of the Bondage Breaker. Praise God! It's as if God had to first tear down the wrong foundations that my sexuality had been built upon, before He could then rebuild me as the sexual man He was calling me to be.

That's what this section of the book is about. We are going to expose several of the sinful sexual roots that I believe hold many Christian men in ongoing struggle and bondage. If these roots are not exposed and properly severed by the power of the Holy Spirit, sexual purity will never be possible. Remember; we are lost at sea and we need a savior. We need Jesus to do for us what we could never do for ourselves. This section of the book is an invitation to repentance. You are invited to consider each one of these "roots" and its corresponding influence in your life. You will then be encouraged to say a prayer of repentance over that particular "root" in your life, and to continue to seek God for the deliverance and freedom that only He can give you. Let's begin by inviting God into our hearts and lives and asking Him for the gift of repentance.

Note: you are invited to say the following prayer from your heart to God, but know the sequence of words written in this prayer, or any other prayer in this book holds no power to change your life. The power to change your life will be determined by the true stature of your heart before God (Luke 18:13-14). If you are only saying words from your head, the words will be powerless. But if you are saying words from a sincere and humble heart that is seeking God to the best of your ability, the words will be powerful. If you are not exactly sure where your heart currently is before God, I encourage you to say the prayer anyway. Be completely honest with God. You might admit to Him that the words feel like they are coming from your head, but you want them to come from your heart. Ask God to help you. Ask God to change your heart. Ask God to do for you what you cannot do for yourself, and He will hear you.

A Prayer for the Gift of Repentance

Dear Heavenly Father, I bring my heart, my life, and my sexuality before you, and I lay them at your feet. I pray that you would grant to me a heart of true and deep repentance. I know that if I am to walk intimately with you in freedom from sin, Lord, I must step from places of darkness and lies in my life to places of light and truth. I pray you would reveal to me the reality of my sin and help me to agree with your full assessment of my true moral and spiritual condition. I pray you would deliver me from any tendency I have to minimize, justify, or rationalize my sin. Lord, you say in your Word that "the sacrifices of God are a broken spirit; a broken and contrite heart, oh God, you will not despise" (Psalm 51:17). I pray you would create within me the sacrifices of a broken and contrite heart, and that the stature of my heart before you would be pleasing to you, oh God. You say in your Word that "God opposes the proud but gives grace to the humble... Humble yourselves before the Lord, and he will lift you up" (James 4:6, 10). I pray, Lord, that you reveal to me any area of my life where you are opposing me because of my sin, and help me to humble myself before you so you can lift me up.

Heavenly Father, I confess that I am a man who has fallen overboard. When I consider the standard of sexual purity you have presented in your holy Word, I know that I have fallen short and have deeply failed in many ways. I confess that I am completely and utterly incapable of changing my own heart, and I pray that you would do for me what I could never do for myself. I pray according to Ezekiel 11 that you would give me an undivided heart and put a new spirit within me, and that you would remove my heart of stone and replace it with a heart of flesh. I pray that Jesus would unleash His redemptive ministry in my life. I pray according to Isaiah 61 that He would bind up my brokenness, proclaim freedom for my captivity, and release me from the darkness of my prisons. I pray according to Isaiah 45 that He would break down gates of bronze in my life and cut through bars of iron. I pray that the Holy Spirit would reveal to me any sinful sexual roots in my life that continue to produce the fruit of sexual sin. I pray, oh God, that you would sever those roots once and for all, and that my life would become holy, pure, and pleasing to you, Lord. I know that purity is your will for my life. I know you are preparing a radiant bride who is "without stain or wrinkle, or any other blemish, but holy and blameless" (Ephesians 5:27). Heavenly Father, it is my desire to honor you with the very areas of my life where I have dishonored you for so long. I pray that my life will bring maximum glory to you, oh God, and maximum insult to the kingdom of darkness. In the Name of Jesus I say that the enemy has held me in places of captivity for long enough. I pray the blood of Jesus would completely cover my heart, my life, my sin, my past, my future, and my sexuality. I pray, oh God, that you would speak deeply into my heart and life. I pray that you would bring me into deeper levels of repentance and freedom than I have ever known. I pray that I would be completely delivered from any bondages that continue to hold me in captivity, and I pray that you would raise me up as the warrior poet you have called me to be, so I can accomplish exploits in your kingdom, oh God, and accomplish your plan and purposes for my life. In the Name of Jesus I pray that you would rebuke the enemy from my life and I give my life completely to you, oh God.

Feel free to add any words or prayers from your heart to God.

Chapter 4

Pornography

Little Boys & Dirty Books

When I was 10 or 11 years old, one of the most significant and harmful events of my life occurred: I discovered my father's pornography. Although most men have a dangerous tendency to minimize the effect pornography has had upon them, with thoughts like, "What's the big deal? Every boy finds pornography. It's just part of growing up." It's interesting to me that virtually every man I talk to about this subject can instantly recall his first exposure to pornography: where he was, who was there, who showed it to him, and how it made him feel. I believe the fact that most of us can so vividly remember the experience says something about the significance of the event upon our young hearts and souls. In my case, there was an immediate, powerful, and overwhelming attraction to the pornography I discovered. I can remember sitting on my mom and dad's bed with numerous magazines lying open all around me, as I literally surrounded myself with the colorful pictures of naked women. Once I made my secret discovery, and knew where the magazines and books were hiding in my father's bedroom, I snuck as often as I could to rendezvous with them. My mom and dad were both gone from home rather frequently, and the solitude of such occasions provided the perfect opportunity for me to feed my hungry eyes. It's as if the magazines and books exerted a strange and mystical power over me, and I almost always heard their silent whispers calling out to me, "Tony, we're waiting for you. Come on, Tony. Come and look at us. You know you like to look at us, so what are you waiting for? Hurry up! Sneak! Come and see!"

In retrospect, I'm really amazed at how much power the pornography exerted upon me at such a young age, and I think it did so for several different reasons.

- I had a natural curiosity that compelled me to investigate.
- I had a kind of emotional "neediness" in my life and the pornography somehow provided a substitute for the genuine and legitimate desires that lived in my young heart. I was hungry to be loved. I was hungry for a sense of intimacy with others. I was hungry for a kind of emotional affirmation and connection from others. In an odd way the pornography was providing for me emotionally in ways I didn't even understand.
- It literally provided a "chemical" experience for my young body that felt good. Of course, I didn't drink alcohol or do drugs at such a young age, and I didn't even know my physical body could be affected by chemical release or reaction, but I believe it was. Without even understanding what was going on, I was drawn further toward the pornography because of how it made me feel.
- The temptation exerted upon me was amplified by the close proximity of the pornography to my life. It was in my house. It was only a few steps away at any given time. It was accessible, and such accessibility added to the constant temptation. If the pornography would have been at a friend's house, for example, I don't think it would have exerted such an unending temptation upon me because it would not have been as "in my face."
- Finally, I believe there was a significant level of spiritual activity occurring around these events. I do not believe it was an accident I found the pornography when I did, and I believe the enemy, with malicious intent and design against me, was literally assaulting my life at this early age in order to ensnare my soul in bondage as quickly as possible. Remember, his goal is to destroy human lives, and I believe he set his sights on me early through the power of pornography.

Soft Concrete & Permanent Impressions

Guys, I think we need to be very careful before we dismiss the significance early exposure to pornography may have had upon us. In his book, *Bringing Up Boys*, Dr. Dobson writes the following and very sobering warning.

I hope you will read very carefully what I am about to write now, because it explains why this matter is so significant. Porn and smut pose an awesome threat to your boys. A single exposure to it by some thirteen- to fifteen-year-olds is all that is required to create an addiction that will hold them in bondage for a lifetime. It is more addictive than cocaine or heroine. That was one of the conclusions drawn during the Attorney General's Commission on Pornography, on which I served. It is known by those of us in the field of child development that the focal point of sexual interest is not very well established among young adolescents. It can be redirected by an early sexual experience (wanted or unwanted) or by exposure to pornography. A boy who would normally be stimulated by a "cheerleader" image of the opposite sex can learn through obscenity to find excitement in hurting someone, or in sex with animals, or in homosexual violence, or in having sex with younger children. Many men who have succumbed to these perverse sexual appetites have traced them to the dawn of their adolescence.[1]

When I reflect upon Dr. Dobson's observations in this quote, I picture in my mind's eye a freshly poured concrete slab. For a rather brief period of time, before the concrete sets up and becomes hard, it remains very soft and impressionable. If during this impressionable period you wrote your initials in the concrete, or pressed something into the surface of the concrete — like your hands or feet — an imprint would remain forever embedded in the surface. In the same way, apparently the sexuality of young boys is very impressionable, and a boy's early exposure to pornography or any variety of sexual experiences can have a dramatic impact that will leave an "imprint," thus significantly affecting that boy's sexuality for years to come. Dr. Dobson says a single exposure is all that is necessary to create an addiction that will hold many adolescent boys for a lifetime. Wow! Could it be that we have seriously underestimated the damage that was done to our own young hearts and sexuality through the power of pornography?

The following two quotes reaffirm that when an adult continues to struggle with his sexuality, the roots of the problem can often be traced to his earliest sexual experiences, including exposure to pornography.

I found that nearly all of my adult sexual addicts' problems started with porn exposure in childhood or adolescence (8 years and older). The typical pattern was exposure to mild porn early with increased frequency of exposure and eventual later addiction. This was nearly always accompanied by masturbation.[2]

In *Pure Desire*, Ted Roberts writes:

> We are awash in a sea of pornography, and the waves are only getting higher. The average age of a first-time viewer of pornography is now down to 11. It will drop even lower in the future because of the flood of porn that is coming through the Internet. Bondage to pornography is seldom something that develops later in life. Usually the seed is planted at a very early age, and by the time of young adulthood its tentacles have been deeply rooted into the person's mind.[3]

Early Fruit

In my own life I can see how the power of pornography influenced the development of my sexuality from the very beginning. In fact, the very awakening of my sexuality and the very first sexual feelings I experienced were the direct results of pornography. If my sexuality was a kind of tree, it's as if the very first fruitful buds that began sprouting on the young tree were the direct result of the pornography. I believe the pornography and the corresponding feelings it provoked inside me made me feel more "alive" than anything else I had experienced to that point in my young life. Something that my heart was hungry for seemed mysteriously nourished by the colorful pictures and detailed stories I was repeatedly exposed to, and if my heart had a voice, it's as if it was saying, "I don't know what it is about this stuff, but it makes me feel so good. I really like it and I want more of it." I believe the pornography provoked an inordinately early sexual awakening in my life. It robbed me of my boyish innocence and stirred sexual feelings in me earlier than normal. It caused me to begin seeing and relating to girls as sexual objects. It provoked an impure thought-life in my mind, and it stimulated sexual feelings in me that were way too big for such a young boy to deal with.

I believe the natural process of adolescence is already tough enough for boys without the added pressure and confusion something like pornography adds to the mix. Young boys already have enough to deal with, including puberty, testosterone, pimples, insecurity, squeaky voices, body hair, and the natural "flame" of sexuality that is beginning to burn in their lives. If you are smart, you know not to start a campfire with gasoline. It's way too explosive and can lead to injury that can last a lifetime. But that's exactly what pornography does to a young boy's heart. How sad that boys can be robbed of their innocence at such an early age, their sexual awakening governed by such impure and unholy influences. Then, adding insult to injury, the enemy dares to whisper in our ears that what happened to us was really no big deal. Well guess what, devil? What happened to us through the influence of pornography is a big deal, but by the power of Jesus we are repenting. Your lie is being exposed. The authority of Jesus is shattering forever the root and power of pornography over our lives!

Controlling Your Eyes

The Bible has a lot to say about what we allow our eyes to see.

- I will set before my *eyes* no vile thing. Psalm 101:3-4
- I made a covenant with my *eyes* not to look lustfully at a girl. Job 31:1
- Let your *eyes* look straight ahead, fix your gaze directly before you. Proverbs 4:25
- A discerning man keeps wisdom in full view, but a fool's *eyes* wander to the ends of the earth. Proverbs 17:24
- You have heard that it was said, 'Do not commit adultery.' But I tell you that anyone who *looks* at a woman lustfully has already committed adultery with her in his heart. If your right *eye* causes you to sin, gouge it out and throw it away. It is better for you to lose one part of your body than for your whole body to be thrown into hell. Matthew 5:27-29
- Death and destruction are never satisfied, and neither are the *eyes* of man. Proverbs 27:20
- One evening David got up from his bed and walked around on the roof of the palace. From the roof he *saw* a woman bathing. The woman was very beautiful, and David sent someone to find out about her. II Samuel 11:2-3

In the last scripture quoted, David *saw* a beautiful woman bathing, and it led to his greatest moral failure when he committed adultery with Bathsheba and then murdered her husband Uriah. Just think of what it took for the enemy to bring down David, the man after God's own heart. The enemy couldn't bring David down through Goliath (I Samuel 17). He couldn't bring David down through the paw of a ferocious bear or a fierce lion (I Samuel 17:34-37). He couldn't bring David down through the wrath of a jealous King Saul (I Samuel 18:10-11). He couldn't even bring David down through the kingdoms he battled in war, including the Philistines, the Amalekites, the Moabites, or the Ammonites (II Samuel 8:6). No, none of these things were able to defeat the great man of God. But what did eventually defeat him and cause the greatest moral failure of his life was his sexuality, and it all began when David *saw* something he was not supposed to be looking at with his eyes.

Why do you think God warns us over and over again to be so careful about what we allow our eyes to see? I believe God knows that our eyes are a kind of gateway to our hearts, and if we look at something long enough our willpower will be weakened, and we will be more likely to yield to the temptation in front of us. In the Garden of Eden "…the woman saw that the fruit of the tree was good for food and pleasing to the eye, and also desirable for gaining wisdom, [so] she took some and ate it" (Genesis 3:6). Seeing leads to taking; that's why God tells us to so carefully guard our eyes and then to quickly flee when we do see temptation in front of us (I Corinthians 6:18).

A Young Boy You Know

As I've already mentioned, many men tend to minimize the harmful things that happened to them during their childhood, including exposure to pornography. In fact, you may be one of those men who finds it hard to discover a heart of sorrow concerning the harmful things that came into your life as a youngster, including exposure to pornography. But imagine if you will, another young boy (age 6 to 16) you might know and love. It could be your own son, your younger brother, a cousin, or even a friend's child. For me, I think of my youngest son, Sammy, who is only 8 years old at the time of this writing.

Picture in your mind's eye how much you love this boy. Picture his innocence and God-given purity at such a young age. Picture him romping and playing and doing the things little boys do. And then picture someone deliberately introducing this young boy to the influence and power of pornography. Imagine for example, that when he goes over his friend's house to play, that an older boy in that house purposely exposes him to pornography, or an adult carelessly leaves pornography out for him to discover and access. Imagine how this event would affect the innocence and purity of the young boy you love. Imagine how it would affect the energy in his young heart toward the opposite sex. Imagine how sad it would be for the earliest stirrings of his sexuality to be in response to such impure and unholy influences. And try to imagine how such an event might affect the ongoing development of his sexuality for literally years to come.

I don't know about you, but the thought of such a terrible thing happening to my son, whom I love and care for so much, deeply grieves my heart. In part, because I know how much I have struggled with my own sexuality as the result of pornography, among many other factors. Because of my own pain and struggle, my desire is to protect my son from such impure influences and to guard his innocence as long as possible. I know we live in a fallen world, and it is impossible to guard our children from the temptations that will inevitably come into their lives. But surely it is right for us to watch over them and provide a protective covering for them as long as possible as they grow in their knowledge and experience with God.

During my process of therapy, my counselor told me one day that I should go to a funeral in my heart: the funeral of a little boy who suffered great loss and experienced a kind of death. Of course, this little boy was me. Although it was difficult for me to understand exactly what he meant at the time, I slowly learned through my healing process to grieve the many ways my life had been harmed as a child, and the things I lost as a result. In time, my heart, which had been so hard, slowly began coming back to life, and I was able to weep over the tragic things that happened to me as a child. I learned to weep over the innocence that was stolen from me; to weep over the assault of the evil one whose diabolical plan to sabotage my life was set in motion against me at such an early age; and to weep for how deeply I was failed by my God-given authorities — namely my father and mother — inadvertently allowing such harmful influences into my life.

Connecting the Dots

Remember, fruit is always the result of roots. Maybe it has never occurred to you before, but maybe the fruit of sexual sin that you continue to struggle with in your life even today could be traced all the way back to a root of pornography. Like me, maybe the earliest sexual stirrings in your life were surrounded by the impurity and ungodliness of pornography. Maybe long ago when you were just a young boy this tiny root began groping its way into your heart, and without your knowledge or understanding, the root somehow took a deep hold on something inside of you and to this day it still has not let go. As you have read this chapter, maybe for the first time you can begin to see — kind of like connecting the dots — how the man you are today is still somehow connected to that young boy who was influenced in such an ungodly way so long ago. I believe we would be deeply shocked if we could really comprehend just how close the two are still connected.

In the following prayer you will be invited to submit this area of your life completely to God. You will ask God to do for you what you could never do for yourself, as you ask Him to completely shatter the root and power of pornography in your life. Are you willing to pray from your heart the following prayer over the power and influence pornography has exerted upon your life?

A Prayer Over the Power and Influence of Pornography

Dear Heavenly Father, I come to you now in the Name of Jesus and I submit my life completely to you. I am beginning to see and understand more clearly than ever how deeply my life and my sexuality have been affected by the power of pornography. I recognize that my early experiences with pornography almost certainly had a profound impact upon my life and left an imprint upon me that has contributed to my ongoing sexual struggles. Heavenly Father, it is my desire to do your will and to bring glory to you through my sexuality. I pray, oh God, in the Name of Jesus that you would cover my life and my sexuality with the blood of Jesus. I pray that you would do for me what I could never do for myself. I pray that you bring freedom, release, and victory to the sexual area of my life like I have never known. I pray over my past, and I specifically pray over the "root" of pornography in my life. I pray that you rebuke and break any power, authority, influence, attachment, or stronghold that exists in my life because of the root of pornography. I pray in the Name of Jesus against any invisible chains or bondages that are attached to my soul because of the root of pornography. I pray, oh God, that you would break the root of pornography in my life that reaches all the way into my past, and that you would cause any "fruit" in my life that still exists because of this unholy root to die, wither up, and blow away. You have said in your Word, oh God, that if I resist the devil he will flee from me. I say now in the Name of Jesus that I resist the devil and command him to flee from my life. I pray that where there has been bondage in my life you would bring freedom. I pray that where there has been darkness in my life you would bring light. I pray that where there has been blindness in my life you would bring sight. I pray that where there has been death in my life you would bring life. I pray according to your Word that you would lift up every valley that lies before me and make low every mountain. I pray that you would make a level path for my feet to travel from this day forward. Heavenly Father, in the Name of Jesus I submit my life to you, and I give you praise for who you are and for what you have done as you break this chain of bondage off my life and set me free from any power pornography holds over me. In the Name of Jesus I renounce pornography from my life. I renounce its power, influence, and authority. I say by faith that the Name of Jesus is more powerful than the name of pornography, and I speak the Name of Jesus over my past, present, and future. Thank you, oh God, for doing for me what I could never do for myself. Thank you for breaking the power of pornography in my life and for setting me free from this chain of bondage. I love you, oh God; I praise you, oh God; and I pray these things in the mighty Name of my Lord and Savior, Jesus Christ.

Feel free to add any words or prayers from your heart to God.

---

1 *Bringing Up Boys,* Dr. James Dobson, Tyndale House Publishers, Inc., 2001, page 209.

2 Dr. Victor B. Cline, *Treatment and Healing of Sexual and Pornographic Addictions.* See www.moralityinmedia.org/pornsEffects/vbctreat.htm

3 *Pure Desire*, Ted Roberts, Regal Books, 1999, page 69.

CHAPTER 5

Role Models

Note: As you read this chapter, reflect upon your memory of your father and/or the other significant male role model(s) in your life: brothers, cousins, friends, uncles, neighbors, teachers, etc.

Father Power

Fathers have enormous power in the lives of their sons. That's the way God set it up. Boys learn how to be men through a process, where they systematically observe and absorb "maleness" from their fathers' examples. By watching dad, and other significant male role models, boys slowly learn what it means to be men: what men think about, what men talk about, what activities men engage in, and what attitudes men should have concerning any given subject. I remember having an argument with some kids in our neighborhood when I was a young boy. They said the Republicans were the best and I said the Democrats were the best. Of course, I didn't have any idea what the real difference was, but I knew my dad was a Democrat, and he didn't like the Republicans at all. I somehow intuitively trusted my father and I wanted to be like him. I knew in my young heart that if my dad said the Democrats were the best that they must be, because my dad certainly couldn't be wrong! Such is the nature of "father power" in the life of a boy.

Dads & Boys & Necklaces

The reality of father power was dramatically illustrated to me once through the behavior of my then 7-year-old son, Sammy. One Saturday afternoon I took Sammy and one of his buddies to a church dinner and carnival. As the three of us walked around the fair, I discovered a booth selling beautiful sterling silver jewelry from Greece. Since my wife loves silver, I picked out a beautiful necklace for her as a surprise. We continued and the boys systematically collected various prizes as they played a variety of games and challenges on the fairway. As we neared the end of the afternoon and it was almost time to leave, Sammy had one ticket left to redeem for the prize of his choice. I thought surely he would go for one more squirt gun, since his friend had a total of three and Sammy had only added two to his growing stockpile of prizes. As he reviewed his many choices — a rubber ball, a whistle, a plastic snake, a slinky, an airplane, a car, or a pair of glasses complete with attached fake nose and mustache, among other options — his friend kept encouraging him to choose the ultimate prize: another squirt gun! "Come on, Sam! Get the squirt gun! Get the orange one! I've got three and you've only got two! Get the orange squirt gun and we'll both have three!" As Sammy continued to review his options from the colorful items spread before him, he suddenly asked the attendant, completely unsolicited by me or anyone else, if he could trade his last ticket for one of the bracelets in a small box on the back corner of the table. The lady was obviously surprised and inquired why in the world a little boy would want such a prize. He looked directly at her and said without hesitation, "I want to get a bracelet for my mom!" The lady commented how sweet and thoughtful he was and told Sammy she thought his mommy was lucky to have such a special little boy. He proceeded to make his selection, and as we walked away, while I felt a sense of pride in the stature of my young son's heart, I also had a sense of trepidation as I realized that he was watching and learning from my example how to treat the women in his life. We made our way home, and my wife became the proud recipient of one beautiful sterling silver necklace from Greece, and in my opinion, an even more beautiful toy bracelet. Wow! Apparently little boys really do watch and learn from their dads — even when dads are unaware they're being watched and sons are unaware they're learning.

What the Experts Say

The significance of father power is mentioned repeatedly through the voice of many experts as they discuss the primary role fathers have in the lives of their sons. In *Bringing Up Boys*, Dr. Dobson says:

If character training is a primary goal of parenting, and I believe it is, then the best way to instill it is through the demeanor and behavior of a father. Identification with him is a far more efficient teacher than lecturing, scolding, punishing, bribing, and cajoling. Boys watch their dads intently, noting every minor detail of behavior and values...So much depends on what they observe in you, for better or for worse... Children may not remember what you say, but they are usually impacted for life by what you do.[1]

In *Wild At Heart*, John Eldredge says:

...you must understand the central truth of a boy's journey to manhood: masculinity is bestowed. A boy learns who he is and what he's got from a man, or the company of men. He cannot learn it any other place. He cannot learn it from other boys, and he cannot learn it from the world of women. The plan from the beginning of time was that his father would lay the foundation for a young boy's heart, and pass on to him that essential knowledge and confidence in his strength. Dad would be the first man in his life, and forever the most important man.[2]

In *Dad the Family Counselor*, Dave Simmons tells the beautiful story of his first fox hunt. When he was 15 years old his father woke him up in the middle of the night, pulled him out of bed, and brought him along — completely unannounced — on his very first fox hunt. Upon arrival, Dave watched from the cab of the pickup with fascination as a group of men clumped around the tailgate in the middle of the night and did what fox hunters do: they listened to the dogs run the fox. They didn't talk. They didn't build a fire to keep them warm. They didn't do anything but stand, freeze, and listen. Commenting on this experience, Simmons writes:

Actually, this episode was one of the most significant of my life. It was dad's way of telling me that he loved me and accepted me as a man. He was bringing me into the fellowship of the men of the clan. Nobody, but nobody, went fox hunting with the men — it was the esteemed inner circle of the tribe, the elite. Dad was announcing that he loved me and accepted me as a man. This experience was my rite of passage, and I missed it.[3]

Whether we like it or not, our lives, including our actions, attitudes, words, and sexuality, will powerfully impact our children's lives and the people they eventually become. And our own fathers' influences upon us have powerfully impacted our lives, including our actions, attitudes, words, and sexuality.

Father Power & Sex

If father power is true concerning virtually every other area of life, then it's also true concerning sexuality. Think about it. Who really taught us to be men? Who taught us what masculinity looks like? Who taught us how men should think, talk, and display their emotion? Who taught us how men should think about women, what men should say about women, how men should relate to women, and the kinds of attitudes men should have toward women? Who taught us how to be sexual and how we should express ourselves as sexual men? I know they don't offer classes titled *How to be a Man* for young boys. No, the fact is, young boys learn how to be men from the classroom of life, with their primary teachers being their fathers and other male role models, and they learn most of their lessons when they don't even know they're learning. It's really kind of scary, and you might have to think real hard to figure out the lessons you were taught by whom.

In my life the primary teacher showing me how to be a man and how to be sexual was my father, and unfortunately many of his lessons were very ungodly and harmful. My father was very sexual, and it was not uncommon for him to make sexual comments or jokes and tease and flirt with the women around him. Over the years I often heard him say unbelievably inappropriate things to the women around him at family or social events, and I am aware of at least a couple different situations that made me wonder whether he was cheating on my mother. Without even knowing that I was learning, my father was teaching me lessons like what it means to be a man, the attitudes I should have toward women, how I should act around women, the things I should say to women, and how I should treat women. His example and demonstration of masculinity had a profound impact upon me as my young heart and sexuality were molded. The very foundation of who I was as a sexual man was being laid in my life, and it was not a pretty picture compared to the holy standard of God's Word. My sexuality literally was being built from the ground up, and I was being programmed from the very beginning for sin and failure. How sad!

Unspoken Lessons

I believe the idea of unspoken lessons is profoundly significant, and that most of the lessons a young boy learns about manhood, masculinity, and sexuality are lessons he doesn't even know he is learning. For example, when a boy finds his father's pornography, the voice of a silent teacher speaks into his life, and teaches him unspoken lessons such as:

- It's alright for a man to have pornography. My dad has it, so I guess it's okay.
- Real men look at pornography. My dad is the best man I know, and he has these magazines and books, so I guess I'm supposed to look at this stuff if I'm a real man.
- Lust is okay in the life of a man. When I look at these magazines, the thoughts and feelings provoked in my heart must be okay.
- Fidelity is not important. My wife does not have to be the sole object of my sexual desire and energy. It's alright for me to look at other women and derive sexual pleasure from sources other than my marriage.
- The primary purpose of sex is to please myself. When I look at this stuff, it's just the magazines and me. It's about me being satisfied and getting what I want.
- Various perversions aren't really that bad. I see reflected in the pornography images of men having sex with men, men having sex with children, men having sex with multiple partners at the same time, men having sex with dead bodies, men being violent during sex, and men having sex with animals. I never thought of all this stuff before, but it must be alright because my dad looks at it.
- The real purpose of women is for sex. It's unnecessary to see them and respect them as people, understand their feelings, and cherish them. It's about their bodies pleasing me. It's about them making me feel a certain way through the power of sex.

An acquaintance of mine had sexual intercourse for the first time when he was just 14 years old. His uncle took him to a whorehouse so he could become a "man." No doubt this experience had a profound impact upon the boy and went a long way in teaching him many things he didn't even know he was learning. The boy no doubt looked up to his uncle, and through this experience his uncle was teaching him lessons such as:

- What it means to be a man.
- What the purpose of women is.
- What a man should do with his sexuality when he feels the urge.
- Marriage isn't a requirement for sex.
- Various attitudes and predispositions concerning himself, women, sex, committed relationships, and God — among many other things.

Undoubtedly this sad and misguided event deeply impacted the development of this man's life and sexuality, just as your life has also been impacted by the culmination of your earliest experiences, including the influence of significant role models in your life.

Personal Application

I highly recommend that you do not rush through these ideas too quickly and then dismiss them as irrelevant. Maybe your father was not as overtly sexual as my father was, and maybe he didn't even have pornography in the house, but the fact remains that someone, somewhere was influencing you and teaching you the lessons of manhood, masculinity, and sexuality. If you take the time to contemplate these matters and to sincerely seek God's help on how your life may have been harmed by the influence of ungodly role models, you will be amazed at the insight and understanding you can gain. These insights will help you comprehend how your ongoing struggle to honor God today with your sexuality is still mysteriously linked to the ungodly events and misguided lessons of so many years ago. As clarity of thought and mind comes to you concerning these matters, the Holy Spirit will then be able to break your chains of bondage as you submit these things to the Lordship of Christ, and you will move to higher levels of freedom than ever before. Jesus said, "Then you will know the truth, and the truth will set you free" (John 8:32).

My own healing process was painstakingly slow and at times very confusing. While visiting with my therapist he invariably insisted on reaching into my past to retrieve stories and understanding about the events of my life. I continuously thought, "Why does he always want to talk about the past? What difference does all that stuff make? It was all so long ago. That weird stuff happens to everybody. I don't care about all that junk. I want to deal with the realities of the problems that I'm facing today in my life, my marriage, and my sexuality. Let's forget about the past and deal with today." But my therapist was wise, and he knew the "key" to my present could only be found by opening the "locks" that had been placed on my life in the past.

When I began my process of therapy, I saw my wife's inability to respond to me sexually as her problem, and I wanted her to get fixed. But, over time, as God worked deeply in my heart, I slowly began to comprehend how the sexual wrongness that lived in me as her husband made it hard for my wife to respond to the kind of man I really was. I slowly began to understand that the sinful "fruit" in my life that I had struggled with for so long was the result of sinful "roots" reaching all the way into my childhood, with one significant "root" being the example of masculinity and sexuality that my father had imprinted on me through "father power." I began to see and understand for the first time how deeply the most significant role models in my life, including not only my father, but also my first pastor, who had a sexual affair with my first girlfriend, had impacted my life negatively. (See chapters 9 & 10 in *Stories*.) As I began "connecting the dots" in my life, I grew in my understanding of who I was as a sexual man, how deeply I had been impacted by the role models in my life, and how these things had contributed to my ongoing struggle with my sexuality. It was through this very process of God-led repentance that He slowly began to break the chains of bondage that had held me captive for so long. I was seeing the truth, and the truth was setting me free.

You are invited to pray the following prayer from your heart, specifically over any negative power or influence your role models might have had on you.

A Prayer Over the Power and Influence of Role Models

Dear Heavenly Father, I come to you now in the Name of Jesus, and I lay my life at your feet. I understand that I have been deeply affected by my male role models, most specifically my father. I recognize that my father may have had many good qualities and that he impacted me in many good ways. But I also recognize that I have probably been impacted negatively by my father's example. It is my growing heart, oh God, to honor you completely with my life, and specifically with my sexuality, and so I pray for the blood of Jesus to completely cover this area of my life. In the Name of Jesus I lift up to you the following specific memories I have and the following suspicions I have concerning how my father's example of masculinity and sexuality have affected my life.

_____

_____

_____

_____

_____

(Specifically name any memories or suspicions you may have concerning how your father's example of masculinity and sexuality may have adversely affected your life.)

Oh God, I pray for the blood of Jesus to cover all of these things. I pray in the Name of Jesus against any continued affect, power, or influence of these things in my life since the day they occurred. I pray against the power these things have had in my life, and I pray that you would rebuke them from my life once and for all. I understand that I am completely responsible for my own sinful choices, attitudes, and actions, but I also understand that much of the sinful "fruit" in my life is the direct result of the childhood "roots" in my life, including my relationship with my father and his example and influence. I pray now in Jesus' name that you would break any negative or sinful influence my father has had upon my sexuality. I pray the Holy Spirit would completely chop and sever any sinful "root" in my life so it is no longer capable of producing sinful "fruit" in my life. I say by faith that I have a Heavenly Father, and I pray that you would establish heavenly "roots" to Him; roots that will produce the "fruit" of holiness and righteousness in my life — especially in the sexual area of my life — from this day forward. Thank you, oh God, that it is not up to me to deliver myself from my past, my sin, or my heritage. I ask that you would do for me what I could never do for myself. Thank you, oh God, for breaking the power of sin in my life and for setting me free. I give you all praise, glory, and honor, and I pray these things in the Name of Jesus.

Feel free to add any words or prayers from your heart to God.

----

1 *Bringing Up Boys,* Dr. James Dobson, Tyndale House Publishers, Inc., 2001, page 69.

2 *Wild at Heart,* John Eldredge, Thomas Nelson Publishers, 2001, page 62.

3 *Dad the Family Counselor*, Dave Simmons, Victor Books, 1991, 44.

CHAPTER 6

GENERATIONAL SIN

Generational Sin, Curses, Bondages, & Familiar Spirits

The Bible teaches much about generational sin, curses, bondages, and familiar spirits. It teaches that it is possible for the sins of the forefathers in a family to be passed down to that family's children, grandchildren, and great-grandchildren. Although it might seem almost unfair to the natural mind and difficult to understand how and why this principle is true, within the economy of God's kingdom, generational sin and curses are a sobering reality. I believe I inherited through the power of generational sin a natural weakness and propensity toward sexual sin. I struggled deeply with this bondage to sexual sin, failing repeatedly, until I was finally set free by the power of God that was released in my life through a process of repentance. The good news is that in Jesus we are given all necessary resources to be completely delivered and set free from every bondage, curse, generational sin, or familiar spirit that has any level of attachment to us.

Body, Soul, Spirit

We are triune in nature, because that's the way God made us. We are body, soul, and spirit. Although I am not an expert scientist, psychologist, or theologian, I believe that familial tendencies replicate themselves in each of these three areas.

Body

People in the same family often have similar physical features. For example, members of one family might be short, another family's members might be on the tall side, and yet another family's members might be dark-complect-ed. Even the secular world recognizes that natural tendencies somehow repeat among a family's generations. For example, when considering a prospective client, a life insurance company will inquire about any family history of heart disease, high blood pressure, diabetes, or cancer. Why? Because if any of these conditions existed in the prospective client's physical history, there is a significantly increased probability that they might occur in the client himself. Based upon such information, the insurance company can then accept or reject the application.

I might be wrong, but I bet you can quickly recognize tendencies, char-acteristics, or physical similarities that tend to repeat in virtually any family you know, including your own or your wife's. In my family my brothers and I look very much alike, and people tell us all the time that we sound exact-ly alike and they can't tell us apart over the phone. In my wife's family the entire gang has several similar characteristics, and my wife coughs and clears her throat exactly like her father. It's really weird!

Soul

The soul consists of the mind, will, and emotions. It's that invisible part of your life that expresses itself through your personality, including how you think and feel, your sense of humor, your propensity to take risks, and a thousand other ways. Do you make impulsive buying decisions or do you tend to think, calculate, and compare before you decide? If you could either watch a car race from the grandstand or actually ride in a racecar going around the track, which one would you choose? Would you rather spend an evening all alone reading a good book, spend the same evening with one spe-cial friend, or with a group of people in a social setting? These are all reflec-tions of your "soulishness," and in the same way physical tendencies can repeat themselves in families, so can soulish qualities. For example, one guy might be quiet and reserved like his dad, and another guy might be more the life of the party, like his dad.

Personally, I inherited a love of the outdoors from my father. He loved to hunt and fish, and he included me in his expeditions from the time I was a little boy. It's really the greatest thing we shared, and it provided an ongo-ing opportunity for me to spend time with my dad as we both grew older. In a mystery, my father's love for the outdoors was somehow "imprinted" on my soul, and my life is now a living reflection of my father's life, even though he is now gone.

Spirit

Doesn't it make sense that just as physical and soulish propensities tend to replicate within families, that somehow spiritual propensities would also? It is a mystery, but the Bible clearly teaches that this is true. Not only can the strengths and blessings within people's lives be replicated in their posterity, but somehow their weaknesses, proclivities, and sins can also be reproduced in families, and the very bondages and curses upon the lives of forefathers can reproduce themselves in the lives of their heritage.

A Christian acquaintance of mine is struggling deeply to find freedom from alcoholism. Not only were his father and grandfather alcoholics, but so was his great-grandfather. This is an obvious pattern of generational sin that repeats itself through the curse of alcohol. Clearly a weakness toward alcoholism has somehow attached itself to this family and continues to replicate. I do not believe this is a coincidence. It is a living example of what the Bible teaches when it references generational sin. For example:

> … I, the LORD your God, am a jealous God, punishing [**visiting**] the children for the sin of the fathers to the third and fourth generation of those who hate me, but showing love to a thousand generations of those who love me and keep my commandments. Exodus 20:5-6

> The LORD, the LORD, the compassionate and gracious God, slow to anger, abounding in love and faithfulness, maintaining love to thousands, and forgiving wickedness, rebellion, and sin. Yet he does not leave the guilty unpunished; he punishes [**visits**] the children and their children for the sin of the fathers to the third and fourth generation. Exodus 34:6-7

> The LORD is slow to anger, abounding in love and forgiving sin and rebellion. Yet he does not leave the guilty unpunished; he punishes [**visits**] the children for the sin of the fathers to the third and fourth generation. Numbers 14:18

God clearly says He will punish the children to the third and fourth generation for the sin of the fathers. The word *punishes* in the previous verses is translated *visits* in the King James Version of the Bible, and I think it is a more accurate translation. In other words, God does not directly *punish* children for the sins of their fathers, but He does allow the sins of the fathers to somehow *visit* their children. According to *Strong's Concordance*, the word "visit" in the Hebrew language means "to visit with friendly or hostile intent," and it carries with it the idea of "bestowing, charging to an account, avenging, or making a deposit." It's almost as if God allows the sins of a father's life to somehow be credited to a spiritual account that his children will later be required to pay. Or further, the father's sin becomes something like a down payment on an account that his children will be required to pay off later.

I don't know how this teaching from God's Word affects you, but it is one of the most alarming principles I have ever learned, and it provokes holy fear in my heart. It is disturbing to realize that sin is very serious business. Not only has my life been deeply affected by the sins of my forefathers, but if the Bible is true, and we know it is, the sin I allow in my life will also deeply affect the lives of my children and grandchildren. Wow! It's pretty scary business and it provokes me to push harder into my understanding of spiritual things so I can discover how to break generational bondages and curses off my life, my children's lives, and the lives of future generations. In my life, I want God to break and rebuke the generational tendencies toward sin and create instead generational tendencies toward purity and holiness. Praise God!

As I've already mentioned, I believe I inherited through the power of generational sin a natural weakness and propensity toward sexual sin. I discovered my father's pornography when I was a young boy, and I watched his poor example of manhood and masculinity for years. Through a mysterious process that deeply affected my life, I somehow absorbed my father's weakness toward sexual sin. In much the same way my father's physical image was reflected in my physical body, and his love of the outdoors was replicated in my soul, it seems his tendency toward sexual sin was also reproduced in my spiritual life.

Although I do not fully understand why my father had this weakness, I did gain a glimpse of understanding in the latter years of my grandfather's life. Although I'm not privy to many details about my grandfather's sexuality, I did learn that he secretly subscribed to pornographic cable channels — even when he was over 90 years old! Although incapable of getting an erection, he apparently delighted in watching pornographic television. I'm not exactly sure of the significance of this information, but it does make me wonder about who my grandfather was as a sexual man. If he was so inclined to pursue such sexual expression in his final years, at such a senior age, it makes me wonder what kind of sexual energy must have lived in his life when he was younger. Although I can't build a foolproof case on this information, it does help me understand a little more of how my father's life and sexuality may have been affected by his father, and it helps me to recognize the tendencies of generational sin in my own family. I believe my grandfather had a sexual weakness in his life that was somehow repeated in my father's life, which was in turn repeated in my life.

A Spiritual Line of Credit

As alluded to previously, it's as though my grandfather opened a kind of spiritual account with the credit card of sexual sin, and as he used this spiritual line of credit, his indebtedness began to grow. My father then inherited the same spiritual account, which no doubt already contained a significant balance. Somehow, within the economy of the spiritual world, the level of credit for my father's generation was significantly increased so he could continue to borrow at higher levels of interest — just as a credit card company starts an account with a lower line of credit and then raises the limit based on increased account activity. By the time I became a young man, inherited the sexual charge card, and started using the same spiritual account passed down from my forefathers, the line of credit had risen so considerably that I could make even larger withdrawals from the account, which I did. The only problem was that my level of accumulated debt was so completely overwhelming that there was no way I could ever break free from the bondage of debt that enslaved me. The result was a kind of spiritual foreclosure.

Just as financial creditors have the right to take things such as furniture or cars away from clients who can't make their payments, it's as if the devil began calling in my line of credit and demanding that I pay in full. When I was completely incapable of paying off the debt resulting from my moral bondage, it's as if the devil said something like, "Fine, if you cannot pay the debt of your sexual sin, I will go ahead and foreclose on your life. I have the right to take away your ministry and your reputation. I have the right to take away your marriage and destroy your children. Your family has been using this line of credit for generations, you owe me big time, and it's time for you to pay!" As the enemy of my soul began to extract this horrible vengeance upon my life, and rightfully so, the weight of my sin, debt, bondage, and complete inability to pay began to crush the very life out of me, and it was only then I began to turn to God in a deeper and more desperate way than ever before. (See the chapter *Divine Desperation* in *Stories*.) As I began to follow Jesus through the subsequent process of repentance He required of me, He began to do for me what I never could have done for myself. Praise God that we have a Savior who loves us, has paid the price of our sin and debt, and can completely save us, deliver us, and set us free from every bondage and generational sin!

Spiritual Authority

When I was a young Christian, I learned the principle of spiritual authority at a Bill Gothard seminar, and I believe the principles of spiritual authority and generational sin are closely related. The truth of spiritual authority can be somewhat pictured using the illustration of an umbrella. Imagine a father walking with his child through a rainstorm. As they walk, the father holds an umbrella over the two of them, and the umbrella protects them both from the falling rain. But imagine what would happen if there was a big hole in one section of the umbrella. The rain would freely fall upon both the father and the child. In this illustration the umbrella represents the covering of divine authority and protection a father is to provide for his children. The rain represents the assault and attack of the destroyer, the devil, upon our lives. When the father has an area of weakness, sin, or bondage in his own life, it's as though he has a hole in that area of spiritual authority and protection over his family. The devil is therefore able to access his life through this area, or hole of weakness, and can therefore also access the children through the same hole. If a man allows pornography and other wrong sexual influences in his life, it's as though he is opening a door that gives various spirits and demons the right to dwell with him. These might include evil spirits that are somehow empowered to exert various sexual temptations like lust, masturbation, and perversion. Since these spirits are allowed access, and further, have the right to exist in the father's home, they will now also have direct access to the hearts of the children in that home. As a result there is the very real possibility that the very areas of weakness, sin, and bondage that existed in the father's life will also be replicated in the children's lives.

This idea is represented by the following two illustrations. When you look at these two illustrations and consider the reality of what they represent, how do you feel, and which of these two illustrations do you want to most represent the reality of your life, family, and children?

WARNING

In no way is this teaching on generational sin intended to give us an excuse for our sins and failures. The Bible clearly teaches that we are each responsible for our own sins. I cannot blame my father, grandfather, or anyone else for the sin in my life or my bad choices. The Bible teaches that I will one day stand before a holy God to give an account for my life, and on that day I will not be able to point a finger of blame to anyone or anything else. I alone will be responsible for my life and my sin, and I alone will answer to God. Therefore, this teaching should not encourage us to have thoughts like, "The reason I struggle with this sin is because of generational sin. It's not really my fault. It's my dad's fault!" Wrong! While it is true that generational sin is a reality that deeply affects our lives, it does not indemnify our sin. Instead, this teaching is intended to help us begin to understand why we may struggle with weaknesses toward certain sins and to enlighten our understanding toward God's solution to the dilemma of generational sin. In Christ, God has provided that solution, and as we repent He is able to break the power of every generational sin, curse, or bondage that has any claim on our lives. We therefore consider this teaching not to find excuses for our lives and our sins, but to find God's deliverance through repentance and obedience.

Where Evil Spirits Dwell

Previously I wrote about the spiritual line of credit my grandfather apparently opened, which was then passed down to my father and then on to me. As each subsequent generation used the account of sexual sin, the level of debt and bondage grew, until it literally almost destroyed my life. It's as though the sin in question was somehow allowed to get progressively worse with each passing generation, which seems to be a biblical principle.

When an evil spirit comes out of a man, it goes through arid places seeking rest and does not find it. Then it says, 'I will return to the house [**family**] I left.' When it arrives, it finds the house unoccupied, swept clean and put in order. Then it goes and takes with it seven other spirits more wicked than itself, and they go in and live there. And the final condition of that man is worse than the first. That is how it will be with this wicked generation. Matthew 12:43-45

In this amazing scripture, according to *Strong's Concordance,* the word "house" literally means "family" or "generations"! Evil spirits apparently do not just live in physical houses; dwellings made with bricks, mortar, and wood; but they can live within the context of *families!* In this particular situation, an evil spirit leaves a family seeking a new place to dwell. After some extended period of time, it is unable to find a new dwelling so it decides to return to its original family. Upon arrival, the spirit finds the *house* swept and clean. It is therefore able to somehow bring in seven other spirits who are even more wicked than itself, leaving the latter generations of the family in even worse shape than the previous generations. Thus, the spiritual condition of that particular family worsens over time as the evil influence and spiritual bondage increases.

I believe this is exactly what happened in my own family. For whatever reasons, I believe my father's life was surrounded by spirits that promoted sensuality, lust, infidelity, and who knows what else. These same spirits were then granted access to my life through the gateway of generational sin. Even though I became a Christian when I was 16 years old, and I tried as hard as I could through self-effort to "sweep, clean, and put my house in order," when the spirits came into my life, they somehow had the right to bring even more spirits with them — which only served to deepen my already severe bondage. It was only after years of struggle, failure, sin, and pain that I finally came to a place of broken repentance, which empowered God to "bind up the strong man" and kick him out of my life and my family forever (Matthew 12:29)!

Familiar Spirits

Not only is the principle of spiritual authority closely related to the reality of generational sin, but so are familiar spirits, which are mentioned repeatedly in the Bible.

Regard not them that have *familiar spirits,* neither seek after wizards, to be defiled by them: I am the LORD your God. Leviticus 19:3, KJV

When thou art come into the land which the LORD thy God giveth thee, thou shalt not learn to do after the abominations of those nations. There shall not be found among you anyone who maketh his son or his daughter pass through the fire, or who useth divination, or an observer of times, or an enchanter, or a witch, or a charmer, or a consulter of *familiar spirits,* or a wizard, or a necromancer. For all that do these things are an abomination unto the LORD; and because of these abominations the LORD thy God doth drive them out from before thee. Deuteronomy 18:9-12, KJV

So Saul died for his transgression, which he committed against the LORD, even against the word of the LORD, which he kept not, and also for asking counsel of one that had a *familiar spirits,* to inquire of her, and inquired not of the LORD; therefore, he slew him, and turned the kingdom unto David, the son of Jesse. I Chronicles 10:13-14, KJV

According to *Strong's Concordance,* in these verses the word translated "familiar" is the Hebrew word "yada," which means "to know, to ascertain by seeing, observation, recognition, to be acquainted with, to be aware of, to comprehend, to discern or discover, to be familiar, to be learned, to be a prognosticator, to have an understanding of." It's really a very amazing word when you understand the implications of its meaning. In other words, a *familiar* spirit is a spirit who knows you. The spirit has ascertained information concerning you based upon observing you and being acquainted with you. This is an alarming thing to realize: evil spirits can know you and be acquainted with your life. Let me try to explain the implications.

As I have already mentioned, I believe my father's life was surrounded by various evil spirits who literally had the right to hang around his life. These spirits of sensuality, lust, adultery, and whatever else, had the right to his soul because he opened himself to their presence and influence through a variety of ways, including among other things, bringing pornography into his home, having immoral friends and associates, and making bad decisions and allowing certain sins in his life. Such factors allowed these evil spirits to attach them-selves to my father's life. I believe these evil spirits were around my father for years, and since they were around him, they were also around me. You see, since I lived with my father, and the evil spirits lived with him, the evil spir-its were also continuously around me from birth. This means they literally watched me grow up. They were around our home throughout my entire childhood: watching me, learning about me, observing me, and literally becoming *familiar* with me. As I became older, they quickly began to attach themselves to my soul, and as I yielded to their influence, they gained more and more power over me. In this way I believe familiar spirits literally attach themselves to families and torment the souls of generation after generation. The result is generational sin.

A Seinfeld Observation

In the popular television series, *Seinfeld,* a common saying on the show was "Yada, yada, yada!" If Elaine said this, what she really meant was, "Yeah, yeah, yeah. I already know that! You don't have to waste your time saying what you are saying right now, because I already know!" Well, guess what? The word "yada" is the same Hebrew word I referenced that is translated *familiar* in the Bible. In fact, we might say the *familiar* spirits talked about in the Bible are really *yada* spirits! This startled me when I realized the impli-cations! It's as though the familiar spirits hanging around my father's life said to one another when I was born and they began watching me, "Yada, yada, yada! We already know about this kid Tony! He's just like his dad! We've been allowed into his grandfather's life, and then his father's life. Now this kid has been born and he's going to be nothing but more of the same! We're going to attach ourselves to his life too, bring bondage and destruction upon him, and then visit his kids and grandkids! Yada, yada, yada!"

Well, guess what? As I have grown in my understanding of these famil-iar "yada" spirits and how they work, I have adopted a heart of offense toward them. How dare they do to my family and me what they have been doing for so many generations! How dare they attach to my life and bring about such bondage and suffering! How dare they try to harm my children and grandchildren! How dare they try to destroy my life! They were wrong when they looked at my life and said to themselves, "Yada, yada, yada! This kid is nothing but more of the same!" They weren't counting on the power of Jesus to find my life, to rescue, redeem, and deliver me forever. They weren't counting on Jesus unleashing His redemptive power in my life and fulfilling the ministry of Isaiah 61 as He would bind up my broken heart, bring freedom to my captivity, and release from my prisons. They weren't counting on Jesus releasing the vengeance of God in my life as He would break down gates of bronze and cut through bars of iron (Isaiah 45:2)! They weren't counting on having to find a new home when they would be rebuked out of my life and the lives of my future generations forever! Praise God! Because of God's grace and mercy, they got more than they bargained for when they messed around with my life, and they're going to get more than they bargained for from your life, too!

Rebuilding Ancient Ruins

Isaiah 61 is the central passage of the Bible that describes the very purpose and ministry of Jesus, and it is the foundational passage of this book. In fact, it's the very passage Jesus chose to quote when He began His public ministry in Luke 4:14-21. The first part of the passage, verses 1-3, which is the part that is most frequently quoted, reveals that the Messiah would be "anointed to preach good news to the poor, bind up the brokenhearted, proclaim freedom for the captives, release from darkness for the prisoners, and the day of God's vengeance." It's a beautiful picture of God's redemptive work in broken lives as He brings comfort to those who mourn, provides provision for those who grieve, bestows a crown of beauty where there have been ashes, and provides a garment of praise where there has been a spirit of despair. It's an exquisite account of God's healing power in shattered lives, but unfortunately most quotations of this passage end with verse 3. This is a real tragedy because verses 4 and following are just as wonderful and exciting as verses 1-3. Next time you read this passage, don't stop at verse 3. Read on and consider the rest of the passage.

> They will rebuild the ancient ruins and restore the places long devastated; they will renew the ruined cities that have been devastated for generations (v. 4).

> Instead of their shame my people will receive a double portion, and instead of disgrace they will rejoice in their inheritance; and so they will inherit a double portion in their land, and everlasting joy will be theirs (v. 7).

> Their descendants will be known among the nations and their offspring among the peoples. All who see them will acknowledge that they are a people the LORD has blessed (v. 9).
>
> For as the soil makes the sprout come up and a garden causes seeds to grow, so the Sovereign LORD will make righteousness and praise spring up before all nations (v. 11).
> Isaiah 61:4-11

Do you realize what this is saying? Do you understand the wonder and power of these words? They offer a beautiful picture of God's ability to redeem the brokenness of our lives, to deliver us from the power of generational ruin, and to begin a new progeny of righteousness through our descendants and future generations! They wonderfully illustrate what God wants to accomplish through our lives. He saves and redeems our lives (v. 1-3), but that is not an end in itself. He doesn't just save us for our own welfare. He not only saves and redeems our lives so we can become trophies of His grace to the display of His splendor (v. 3), but He literally wants to reach *through* our lives into future generations! He promises that through our lives He can *rebuild, restore,* and *renew* the places in our lives that have been devastated for generations (v. 4)! He can remove the shame and disgrace of our inheritance and bestow upon us a double portion of blessing that will empower us to rejoice (v. 7). He promises that our descendants will be known among the nations and that all who see them will acknowledge that these are a people whom the Lord has blessed (v. 9)! It's an awesome picture of God changing the destiny of future generations through our lives. It's an awesome picture of God delivering us from the power of generational sin and initiating through us generations of righteousness that will sprout from the soil of our lives in the same way a garden causes seeds to grow (v. 11). It's an awesome picture of the sovereign Lord making righteousness and praise spring up before all nations through our lives (v. 11)! Praise God! Praise God! Praise God! There is hope in God! There is hope in Christ! He has a plan, a future, and a destiny for our lives! He has the power to heal, deliver, and redeem! He has the power to rebuild, restore, and renew! He has the power to break every generational sin, curse, and bondage off our lives! He has the power to change our lives and to begin generations of righteousness through us that will testify to the entire earth that we are a people whom the Lord has blessed!

Doing Business with God

Imagine you are selling a used car. You're asking $5,000.00 for the car, and after a potential prospect looks at it, he offers you a basket of gravel and ten baskets of leaves in exchange for the car. What would you do? Obviously you would reject his offer. The currency he is offering in exchange for your car is ridiculous, and if he is really serious about buying the car, he needs to bring you the currency you are really interested in: cold, hard cash! If he brings you the correct currency, you will do business with him. So what currency do we need to bring God in order for God to do business with us? What is the currency of God's kingdom? If we are really serious about seeing God move in our lives in a powerful way — to change our lives, to free us from generational sin, to radically renew our sexuality and change our marriages — what can we bring God that will compel Him to move in our lives?

In a mystery, the currency of God's kingdom is very different from the currency of this world. If you want to do business with God, you have to bring God the currency of His kingdom. What does God value? What can you bring God that will compel Him to do business with you? I promise you God is not impressed by how much money you have. He's not interested in your house, or even in your good works. He's not interested in how often you go to church or how much you tithe. If you bring God this kind of currency in the hope that He will respond to you, you will be sadly disappointed. As shown in the following verses, what God is really interested in is the stature of your heart before Him!

> Come, all you who are thirsty, come to the waters; and you who have no money, come, buy and eat! Come, buy wine and milk without money and without cost. Isaiah 55:1

> You do not delight in sacrifice, or I would bring it; you do not take pleasure in burnt offerings. The sacrifices of God are a broken spirit; a broken and contrite heart, O God, you will not despise. Psalm 51:16-17

> God opposes the proud but gives grace to the humble. Submit yourselves, then, to God. Resist the devil, and he will flee from you. Come near to God and he will come near to you. Wash your hands, you sinners, and purify your hearts, you double-minded. Grieve, mourn and wail. Change your laughter to

> mourning and your joy to gloom. Humble yourselves before
> the Lord, and he will lift you up. James 4:6-10

> Blessed are the poor in spirit, for theirs is the kingdom of
> heaven. Matthew 5:3

Apparently the currencies that compel God to unleash His redemptive power in our lives are things like a broken heart and contrite spirit, humility, submission, grief, mourning, wailing, and poverty of spirit. Wow!

Are You Willing to Grieve?

In Isaiah 61, we find the same truth almost hidden in the passage, and if you are not looking for it, you can easily miss the "key" that unlocks the redemptive work of the Messiah in our lives. Notice what characteristics empower Jesus to loose His powerful anointing in the lives of those whom He redeems.

> ...the LORD has anointed me to preach good news to the
> *poor.* He has sent me to bind up the *brokenhearted,* to proclaim
> freedom for the *captives*...to comfort all who *mourn*...and
> provide for those who *grieve* in Zion. Isaiah 61:1-3

In a mystery, God works deeply to deliver and redeem those who are poor, brokenhearted, captive, mourning, and grieving. These are the currencies of the Kingdom, and these are the treasures that will compel God to move powerfully in our lives, to break generational bondages, to change our sexuality, and to make us better men. It's not about self-effort. It's not about us trying harder. It's not about following tips and techniques. It's not about us going to church more or giving more money. It's not about us participating in another accountability group. It's not about us attempting to clean up our lives. IT'S ABOUT REPENTANCE! It's about us finding a broken heart and the "gift of tears." It's about us learning to be poor in spirit. It's about us learning to mourn and grieve. And so I ask...are you willing to grieve?

Nehemiah

Nehemiah is an awesome book in the Bible. It records the story of how God used Nehemiah to rebuild the wall of Jerusalem after the Babylonians invaded Israel and destroyed the holy city. Nehemiah was a slave serving as the cupbearer to King Artaxerxes in a far-away city when several men came from Jerusalem on a journey. When Nehemiah discovered that these men had come from Jerusalem, he questioned them concerning the Jewish remnant that had survived the exile, and also about the city itself. The men gave Nehemiah the devastating news that the exiles were in great trouble and the wall of Jerusalem had been broken down and burned with fire. When Nehemiah heard this terrible news, he did five things that I believe reveal the state of his heart, and further reveal why God chose Nehemiah as the vessel He would use to rebuild the walls of the holy city.

> When I heard these things, I sat down and wept. For some days I mourned and fasted and prayed before the God of heaven. Nehemiah 1:4

Wow! When Nehemiah heard the terrible news concerning Jerusalem, he sat down, wept, mourned, fasted, and prayed. We might say Nehemiah brought God the currency of heaven. I also believe as we learn to bring God the currency of heaven, God will do some serious business in our lives and radically empower us by the Holy Spirit to rise up and accomplish the exploits and purposes for which he has made us (Ephesians 2:10).

Nehemiah and Generational Repentance

As we look closer at the book of Nehemiah, we find the most amazing thing, and something that is almost never talked about in Christian circles. Nehemiah literally confesses and repents on behalf of his forefathers! Take a look at the very first words he prayed to God as he began fasting and mourning.

> O Lord, God of heaven, the great and awesome God, who keeps his covenant of love with those who love him and obey his commands, let your ear be attentive and your eyes open to hear the prayer your servant is praying before you day and night for your servants, the people of Israel. *I confess the sins we Israelites, including myself and my father's house, have committed against you. We have acted wickedly toward you. We have not obeyed the commands, decrees and laws you gave your servant Moses.* Nehemiah 1:5-7

Notice that Nehemiah confessed his own sins, as well as the sins of his people and of his father. Later in the book, after the wall is rebuilt, the prophet Ezra reads the book of the law to the people and a period of corporate repentance follows in which the priests further confess the sins of their forefathers.

> On the twenty-fourth day of the same month, the Israelites gathered together, fasting and wearing sackcloth and having dust on their heads...*they stood in their places and confessed their sins and the wickedness of their fathers...*You saw the suffering of our *forefathers* in Egypt; you heard their cry at the Red Sea...But they, *our forefathers,* became arrogant and stiff-necked, and did not obey your commands. They refused to listen and failed to remember the miracles you performed among them. They became stiff-necked and in their rebellion appointed a leader in order to return to their slavery. But you are a forgiving God, gracious and compassionate, slow to anger and abounding in love. Therefore you did not desert them...But they were disobedient and rebelled against you; they put your law behind their backs. They killed your prophets, who had admonished them in order to turn them back to you; they committed awful blasphemies...Stubbornly they turned their backs on you, became stiff-necked and refused to listen...*Our kings, our leaders, our priests and our fathers...* did not pay attention to your commands or the warnings you gave them. Selections from Nehemiah 9

These are amazing verses! As Nehemiah and the Israelites came face-to-face with the reality of the bondage, captivity, and devastation that confronted them, they entered a process of repentance. That process included, in large part, acknowledgment, confession, and repentance over the sin, disobedience, and rebellion of their forefathers!

They seemed to intuitively know that the dilemma of bondage they found themselves in "today" was somehow inextricably linked to their forefathers' "yesterday." Therefore, they didn't just confess their own sin; they also confessed the sin and rebellion of their fathers.

A Personal Invitation

Maybe it has never occurred to you that the bondages and captivities of your life, including the bondage of your sexual struggles and addictions, could somehow be inextricably linked to your forefathers through the root of generational sin. As you consider the profound implications of this principle, you may begin to recognize sinful lines of credit that have been attached to your family for generations, including anger, controlling spirits, bitterness, unforgiveness, hatred, revenge, violence, manipulation, greed, cruelty, alcoholism, fear, immorality, impurity, sensuality, lust, adultery, homosexuality, perversion, or any other such sexual sin.

As God speaks into your life concerning these things, you are invited to continue walking a pathway of repentance, not just for your own sin, but also for the sins of your forefathers. Are you willing to pray over your heritage and ask God to cover your family history with the blood of Jesus? Are you willing to seek God for deliverance and freedom so He can break every chain, bondage, attachment, or encumbrance that reaches into your family history? Are you willing to turn the tide of generational sin in your family and begin a heritage of righteousness and freedom for future generations?

Are you willing to pray the following prayer from your heart, specifically asking God to break the power of generational sin, curses, and bondages off of your life forever?

A PRAYER TO RENOUNCE CURSES, BONDAGES, & GENERATIONAL SIN

Dear Heavenly Father, you have said in your Word that the sins of the fathers will pass down to the third and fourth generations of children (Exodus 20:5). I understand it is possible to be held captive in places of darkness by invisible chains of curses, bondages, and generational sin that have been allowed into my life through a variety of sources, including my forefathers' sin, rebellion, and disobedience, as well as my own sinful rebellion, disobedience, and actions. I thank you, Father, that you desire to set me free from the dark influences and forces that hold me captive, and you have revealed in your Word that the very ministry of Jesus is to bring freedom to prisoners (Isaiah 61:1). I therefore pray in the powerful Name of Jesus that you would cover every area of my life with the blood of Christ. I know that Jesus died on the cross to set me free and to deliver me from every bondage and curse upon my life, and in Jesus' name I speak the following scriptures over my life.

> It is for freedom that Christ has set us free. Stand firm, then, and do not let yourselves be burdened again by a yoke of slavery. Galatians 5:1

> There is now no condemnation for those who are in Christ Jesus, because through Christ Jesus the law of the Spirit of life set me free from the law of sin and death. Romans 8:1-2

> Christ redeemed us from the curse of the law by becoming a curse for us, for it is written: "Cursed is everyone who is hung on a tree." Galatians 3:13

Lord, it is my desire to experience the freedom you have provided for me, especially in the sexual area of my life. In the Name of Jesus I renounce every bondage, curse, and generational sin that has been granted access to my life through the gateway of my parents and ancestors, and I pray that these powers and influences would be rebuked and broken from my life. Forgive me for any of my sinful words, thoughts, or actions that have contributed to any bondage or stronghold that holds me captive. I renounce any spirit of darkness or influence that has been granted access to my life through my participation or involvement with immoral behavior, people, or places; occultic practices or exposure; or any other exposures I have had to the kingdom of darkness. I pray against all these things, known and unknown, in the Name of Jesus, and I pray that the blood of Jesus would cover and break all these powers in my life. I specifically pray for freedom and release from:

_____

_____

_____

(Name any specific areas of bondages, curses, generational sin, stronghold, or captivity that you are aware of in your family history or that you struggle with personally.)

I pray that every area of darkness and bondage in my life would be brought into the glorious light of Christ. I pray, oh God, that you would turn the tide of generational sin in my life. I pray that you would change the destiny of future generations through my life. I pray you would rebuild in my generation the ancient ruins of my family, and restore the places that have been devastated for generations (Isaiah 61:4). I pray, oh God, that you would break every chain of generational bondage off of my life, and I pray all these things in the mighty and powerful Name of Jesus.

Feel free to add any words or prayers from your heart to God.

CHAPTER 7

SEXUAL ABUSE

The Web of Abuse

Imagine a young child you know and love, perhaps your own son, daughter, niece, or nephew, is secretly being sexually molested at this very time. Perhaps the perpetrator is an older child in the neighborhood, or a "friend" of your family. Perhaps the perpetrator is a relative, someone your child would automatically trust because of who he is, or an admired authority figure in his or her life, like a teacher or a Scout leader.

Imagine for a moment what the web of abuse that ensnares your little one probably looks like.

- The child has natural and God-given needs to be loved and accepted, to be touched and enjoyed.
- The perpetrator has drawn his victim — the child you love — into his diabolical web by being kind and using the child's natural tendency to "trust" against him.
- The perpetrator "sets up" his victim by making him feel special, by giving him treats, and showing him other kinds of favoritism.
- The perpetrator advances his evil cause by establishing a sense of exclusivity and secrecy in the relationship. He might use lines like, "I brought you this candy today, but nobody else can know about it. If your mom finds out, she will be mad, so we can't tell her. It's going to be our secret, and nobody else can know." Or, "We have a secret club, and we are the only members. We are going to play a secret game today, and no one else can be in our club or play our game.

You get to be in the club because you are so special and you are good at keeping secrets."

- The abuse progresses when the perpetrator establishes a pattern of physical intimacy through appropriate forms of touch like hugs, kisses, touching the cheek, and caressing the hair.

- Sexual abuse finally occurs when the physical touch advances from appropriate to inappropriate forms of behavior — perhaps inappropriate language; sexualized kissing; exposing parts of the body for one another to look at; touching private parts of the body; inappropriate oral contact; or even sexual intercourse.

- The perpetrator reaffirms the victim's silence and the opportunity to continue the abuse through a combination of intimidation and privileges.

  - Intimidation — The perpetrator might say, "If you tell anybody about our secret, your mom and dad will be really mad at you and you will get in big trouble."

  - Privileges — The perpetrator might say, "You are such a special little boy. Since you are so good at keeping secrets, I am going to take you for ice cream this week, and I will buy you a new toy. Would you like that?"

We would all like to think that such a terrible thing could never happen to one of our loved ones, but realistically things like this happen all the time. In most situations the perpetrator turns out to be someone least expected: a family friend, a relative, a neighborhood kid, or a person in a position of authority. It's easy to feel a sense of shock and outrage when you imagine the horror of sexual abuse, especially if the victim is someone you love dearly, like a child or a grandchild. But for some strange reason, it's much harder to feel that same sense of shock and outrage when we ourselves were the victims of such abuse. Imagine for a moment the same scenario of abuse outlined above, only this time imagine yourself as the victim!

Male Sexual Abuse

Please be careful before you quickly decide that this topic has nothing to do with you. As part of my own healing process, in addition to meeting with a counselor for an extended period of time, I ended up in a weekly small group that consisted of several men who were all in a similar process of repentance as I was. Participating in this group allowed me to be part of a community of fellow strugglers, and my weekly involvement affirmed I was not alone in my battle. There were other men who, like me, were wrestling deeply with issues such as facing their past, considering their wounded sexuality, contemplating and trying to understand their sin, and struggling with their difficult marriages. Other men who could relate to my battle encouraged me weekly and I drew strength from the group as we prayed for one another, shared our stories and our lives, and held one another accountable. The amazing thing about this group was, when our process began, virtually none of the men believed he had been sexually abused, and it took each man a considerable amount of time to finally realize he was indeed a victim.

Each man had suffered sexual abuse at different ages and in different ways, among others: abused as a child by a teacher, abused by a pastor in a church, abused by older women, abused by a family member, and brutally and violently raped by other men. As we listened to one another's stories, we each readily recognized the obvious abuse of the other men, but virtually without exception, each man had trouble clearly seeing and acknowledging his own sexual abuse. It was through our small group, the process of each man's therapy, and the redemptive touch of God, that we all learned to face the fact that we had suffered indeed as a result of sexual abuse. Before you quickly decide this topic does not relate to your life, please at least consider it.

A Definition

In his book, *The Wounded Heart,* Dr. Dan Allender defines sexual abuse as follows:

> Sexual abuse is any contact or interaction (visual, verbal, or psychological) between a child/adolescent and an adult when the child/adolescent is being used for the sexual stimulation of the perpetrator or any other person. Sexual abuse may be committed by a person under the age of eighteen when that person is either significantly older than the victim or when the perpetrator is in a position of power or control over the victimized child/adolescent.[1]

Understanding the implications of this definition is very significant, so I encourage you to take the time to read and meditate upon it. Do not mistakenly equate sexual abuse only with overt acts of sexual violence or forcible rape. Many men quickly think, "I have never been sexually abused, because I was never raped." But this is a way wrong concept of what sexual abuse really is. The evil one is much smarter than that. He knows that if most of us were, for example, forcibly raped, we could easily recognize the harm that was perpetrated against us. We would then be able to see the issues as black and white, and deal with the harm and resulting consequences accordingly.

No, the evil one would much rather assault our lives by launching his diabolical efforts against us through the grid work of our natural and God-given desires, like mixing poison in grape Kool-Aid. In this way, when we quench our legitimate thirst by drinking from the cup of our abuser, we are deceived into gulping down the poison without even realizing its harm. Later, when we are violently sick, and someone tries to tell us that we have been poisoned, we deny emphatically that we have been poisoned, insisting, "What are you talking about? I've never been sexually abused." By cunningly sneaking the abuse into our lives through the gateway of normal desires, like the desire to be loved and accepted, touched and enjoyed, the evil one creates an amalgamation that is so subtle we are usually unable to recognize the harm that has been leveled against us. The issues are no longer black and white, and in time the poison that we have ingested into our lives through sexual abuse takes its toll through a variety of hidden forces, possibly including shame, contempt, helplessness, lack of trust, and ambivalence. We come to live in a muddled world where everything appears gray and confusing. Through the influence of sexual abuse, the enemy can paralyze our lives and deeply hinder our ability to enjoy healthy and successful relationships with God and with others. We begin to have thoughts like the following, "I long for meaningful relationship and connection with others yet seem incapable of trusting and remain cautiously guarded toward even those closest to me." Or, "I'm able to engage my wife sexually; body to body; but seem unable to engage her emotionally; heart to heart." Or, "I'm not sure I can trust myself or my feelings. It seems like every time I think another person will be good for me, it ends up turning into a disaster. Why am I such a mess?" Surely sexual abuse is one of the devil's most cunning and destructive strategies.

Sexual Abuse?

Consider whether sexual abuse occurred in the following scenarios.

- When he was a boy, Larry attended a week-long youth camp. While at this camp, one of the camp counselors who seemed to really like

Larry exposed himself to Larry repeatedly. The counselor tried to get Larry to do the same thing, which he did not do because he was afraid.

- When Bill was a teenager, he became involved at church for the first time in his life. Bill's father was busy, angry, and distant. The youth pastor showed a special interest in Bill, and the boy soaked up the attention from an older male in much the same way a dry sponge soaks up a spill. In a matter of time, the youth pastor began touching the boy inappropriately, and coerced the boy into touching him in the same way.

- Throughout his childhood, Greg occasionally spent the night at his cousin's house. From where he slept, he had an obvious view of the bathroom across the hallway. It seemed inevitable that almost every night he was there, his aunt left the bathroom door partially open as she showered and got ready for bed. Even though his aunt had a master bathroom, whenever Greg slept over, she showered in the hallway bathroom. It wasn't until years later Greg realized that his aunt was deliberately exposing herself to him.

- Steve and his older brother shared a bedroom. His older brother frequently got in Steve's bed and made his younger brother masturbate him. For years it didn't even occur to Steve that this was wrong behavior, because his brother made him do it for as long as Steve could remember.

- At least once, when John was about 6 years old and his older brother babysat him and a young neighborhood girl, the older brother made the two children take off their clothes. He told them they were playing a game. The older brother positioned the children as if they were having intercourse, but actual intercourse did not occur.

In each of these sad situations, sexual abuse occurred. None of them included violence or force. What's surprising is how many men can recall some kind of similar situation in their life when they were a child/adolescent, but it never occurred to them that they had been sexually abused.

Seductive Women

When I was an adolescent, two different older women in my life sexually abused me. (See chapter 5 in *Stories* for a detailed description of these accounts.) The first situation involved a young lady who was 5 years older than I was. I recount the scene in *Stories* as follows:

> I had a small throw blanket over me, and after some period of time I remember feeling stirred as if someone was trying to quietly wake me up. As I slowly opened my eyes, I realized this girl's arm was draped over the front seat in a way that would not create attention, and her arm was under my blanket as she gently caressed the inside of my thigh and leg with her hand. For a moment I thought she was joking, and I wondered what she was doing. As she continued softly touching me, it slowly began to dawn on me what she was doing, and as it did the realization took my breath away. 33

The other situation involved a married woman who lived in a neighborhood near ours. I was around this woman regularly, and occasionally babysat her two young children. Whenever I was around her, she frequently said and did provocative things, and I didn't understand until years later how completely inappropriate her behavior toward me really was. In *Stories,* I write about one particular incident as follows:

> One night she invited me to go to the drive-in with her and her two children. For whatever reason her husband did not come along, and it was just the four of us. When we got to the drive-in, she made her kids sit outside the car on a blanket to watch the movie, and we stayed in the car. She then invited me to sit next to her in the backseat. She said we should sit together in the middle of the seat so we could see the screen better though the middle of the front bucket seats. I clearly remember what movie we were watching because of what happened next. The movie was *The Godfather.* In one particular portion of the movie, the character Michael — who was the youngest son of gangster Don Corlione — kills two members of an opposing mob family and then flees to Sicily in hiding. While in Sicily he meets and falls in love with a beautiful young Sicilian girl. Through a series of events he ends up marrying her, and a provocative scene occurs on their wedding night. After entering their honeymoon suite, Michael closes the curtains to create an

atmosphere of privacy, and as he turns to approach his new bride, she slowly lets her dress fall off her shoulders to expose her naked beauty to her new husband. It's a breathtaking scene, especially for a 14-year-old boy, let alone in the backseat of a car with a beautiful older woman. As this powerful scene was unfolding on the giant screen in front of us, the woman I was with warmly snuggled next to me, and quietly whispered in my ear, "Would you like it if I took off my shirt for you?" 36

I believe both of these women had a seductive spirit about them, and for whatever reasons they chose to direct their seduction toward me on many different occasions. My suspicion is that the spirits of seduction on these women somehow sensed the sexual weakness that already existed in my life and were attracted to me accordingly. Of course, I don't believe either one of them was sincerely attracted to me or interested in a genuine relationship with me. Instead, it's as if they were cats and I was a mouse they had captured, and they enjoyed the game of teasing, playing, and manipulating me. I'm quite sure their feeling of sensual titillation must have been heightened by my obvious lack of experience, and they must have felt a sense of almost intoxicating power by being the aggressors. Of course, these situations in my life were clearly abusive since I was being used to provide a sense of sexual stimulation for my perpetrators.

Consequences

For many years of my life, if you had asked me if I was the victim of sexual abuse, I would have said no. I did not know that I had been sexually abused, and I had no idea that my life and my sexuality had been deeply impacted by the things that had happened to me. What I did know was that I had great difficulty controlling my sexuality in a way that was honoring to God, and my marriage and my sexual relationship with my wife were complete disasters. As I struggled deeply with the sinful "fruit" that continually manifested itself in my life, I couldn't understand that the current realities of my life were mysteriously connected to the "roots" that reached far into my past, and that one of those roots was the root of sexual abuse. As I continued to walk the pathway of repentance I was slowly discovering, God spoke into my life through a variety of "voices," including my therapy process, books, and the small group of men I was involved with. It was through these various voices that I slowly began to comprehend the damage that had been done to my life and to my sexuality, and with each new level of understanding and clarity I was able to repent accordingly, which led to greater levels of freedom in my life.

Ultimately the real problem of sexual abuse is how it continues affecting our lives and relationships in ways we don't even realize. In my case, the sexual abuse compounded and reinforced the wrong sexual "energy" that was already present in my young soul as a result of the following: pornography, my father's example of masculinity, my bondage to masturbation, the power of generational sin, and the natural tendency of my own sinful flesh. These seductive women and their abuse against me — sadly — represented my first sensual encounters with the opposite sex. These situations of sexual abuse "taught" me lessons I didn't even know I was learning, and "shouted" messages to me like billboards along the highway of my sexual development. Messages like:

- Real women are just like the women in the magazines and books. They are sensual, sexual, suggestive, and nasty.
- Relationships with women are not about love, respect, and kindness. They are about lust, desire, and passion.
- I should serve lust and desire regardless of proper boundaries. For example, it's okay for a married person to flirt with someone other than his or her spouse. It's alright if someone in a committed relationship toys sexually with someone other than his or her significant other.
- The lessons my father taught me concerning women must be true. Women are sexual objects that want to be treated sexually.

In a strange way it's as if my sexual abuse had a voice that spoke powerfully into my life, and the messages it taught me were very destructive — reinforcing the wrong direction my sexuality was already taking.

Note: Understanding the significance of how deeply our lives were and continue to be affected by sexual abuse is a process that unfolds over time. For me, this process included going through extended therapy, participating in small groups, and reading several books. I am not currently a professional therapist, and I am not equipped to help people with such an extensive process. It is my hope that this chapter has introduced you to the reality of sexual abuse and its devastating effects, and has helped you to identify such abuse if it has occurred in your life. If you sense that you have further business to do with God regarding sexual abuse, I highly suggest you begin by reading *The Wounded Heart* by Dr. Dan Allender and by seeking the professional guidance of a Christian therapist.

Are you willing to pray the following prayers from your heart as you seek God's healing touch in your life? The first prayer is designed to release you from all harm perpetrated against you through sexual abuse, and the second prayer is designed for the release and freedom of your own soul as you pray for forgiveness toward those who have harmed you.

A Prayer for Release from All Harm Perpetrated Against Me

Dear Heavenly Father, in the Name of Jesus I speak the following scriptures over my life.

> No weapon forged against you will prevail, and you will refute every tongue that accuses you. Isaiah 54:17

> You intended to harm me, but God intended it for good to accomplish what is now being done, the saving of many lives. Genesis 50:20

> Therefore, if anyone is in Christ, he is a new creation; the old has gone, the new has come! I Corinthians 5:17

Heavenly Father, there is an enemy of my soul who has attempted to destroy my life through terrible and abusive past events. My life has been deeply harmed by these sad events that were perpetrated against me. These events include:

_____

_____

_____

(Individually name any persons who harmed you or past events by which your life was harmed, including circumstances that negatively

influenced the development of your sexuality. **This might include intro-
ductions and exposures to pornography or immoral behaviors, situations of sexual abuse or rape, failures of those in positions of authority
in your life, or any other harmful persons or situations you can recall.)**

Heavenly Father, I lift up to you each one of these people and situations
that have caused harm in my life. I lay these people and these events at your
feet, and I pray that you would cover each one of them with the blood of
Jesus. I know that my life has been adversely affected by these things, and
they have contributed to the negative direction and shaping of my sexuality
and my life. It is my desire to be set free from any remaining power or influence these events continue to hold over my life, and in the Name of Jesus, I
pray that you would rebuke and renounce every power, influence, attachment,
or effect they continue to have upon me. Lord, you have said in your holy
Word, "If the Son sets you free, you will be free indeed" (John 8:36). I pray
in Jesus' name that you would set me free from every curse, bondage, stronghold, or hindrance that is attached to my life in any way as the result of these
dark and harmful things that were perpetrated against me.

I pray in Jesus' name that every weapon ever formed against me in the
attempt to hinder or destroy my life would be rebuked and rendered powerless from this day forward (Isaiah 54:17). I pray that you would rebuke what
the enemy intended to harm my life with and pray that you would turn those
things to my good and the saving of my life (Genesis 50:20). I pray the divine
power of God would be released to demolish all strongholds in my life and
that old things would be put to death as God's life is allowed to burst forth in
newness and power (II Corinthians 10:3-4). In the Name of Jesus I say that
the power of my past and the power of every weapon formed against me is
broken, and the power of God is released in my life to enable me to live in
freedom and newness of life. I thank you and I praise you, God, for the victory
and freedom I have in Christ, and I pray these things in the Name of Jesus.

Feel free to add any words or prayers from your heart to God.

A PRAYER OF FORGIVENESS

Dear Heavenly Father, I come to you today seeking a heart of forgiveness
toward every person who has harmed my life in any way, and especially those
who have sexually abused me. I know your desire for me is to have a heart

of forgiveness toward these people, and that any resentment, bitterness, or unforgiveness that lives in my heart is like a cancer that is displeasing to you and only continues to imprison me. I confess that I am weak and powerless in my ability to change my own heart, and I am asking you to do for me what I cannot do for myself. It is my desire to have a heart that is pleasing to you and to walk in freedom before you and others. I recognize that forgiveness is not an event. It is not something I do one time only and then never struggle with again. I am asking you to help me forgive those who have harmed me, offended me, or violated me, and I am asking you to help me walk in forgiveness toward each of them in the days ahead.

Heavenly Father, I know that in the same way these people need forgiveness, I also need forgiveness. I am a sinner and I have failed, hurt, betrayed, and harmed many people in my life, including some of those closest to me. I realize there are people in this world perhaps struggling as they try to find forgiveness in their hearts toward me because of how I have hurt them. I am therefore in desperate need of mercy and forgiveness from these people and from you. I know that of all the people I have hurt by my sin, I have hurt and grieved you the very most because you are a holy God. I therefore pray as David prayed: "Have mercy on me, O God, according to your unfailing love; according to your great compassion blot out my transgressions. Wash away all my iniquity and cleanse me from my sin" (Psalm 51:1-2).

Lord, as I remember my own desperate need to be forgiven, it becomes easier for me to find a heart of forgiveness toward those who have sinned against me. From such a place of need I commit each one of the following situations and memories to you, and I pray that you would help me to forgive the following people who have sinned against me and harmed my life. I say by faith in the Name of Jesus that I choose to forgive:

_____

_____

_____

(Individually name each person you need to forgive as well as the sin he or she committed against you.)

Lord, I pray you would remove from my heart any desire for revenge or any longing to see these people pay for their wrongs done to me. I know I have no right to judge any other person, and I do not have the understanding or wisdom to do so properly. I know that you see the hearts of all men, and you alone have the right to perfectly judge each person. I therefore release these people to you, revoking any right I have for revenge, and trusting that you are a big enough God to take care of each situation with perfect wisdom, equity, and righteousness according to your perfect will and plan. In the Name of Jesus I forgive each one of these people for the harm he or she has caused in my life. I lay each one of these people and situations at your feet, Lord, and I pray that you would set me free from any burden or bondage that exists in my life as a result of these things. I pray the blood of Jesus would cover each one of these situations.

Lord, I thank you and praise you for how you are working in my life. I thank you that I do not have to remain in bondage to my past or the evil things that have been perpetrated against me. I thank you and praise you that you have made a way for me to be set free through Jesus, and through your power in my life I can be forgiven and I can forgive those who have hurt me. In the Name of Jesus I speak forgiveness and release both in my life and toward all those who have sinned against me.

Feel free to add any words or prayers from your heart to God.

---

1 *The Wounded Heart,* Dr. Dan Allender, NavPress, 1990, page 30.

CHAPTER 8

THE FLESH

The Tasmanian Devil

For years of my life it seemed like a fierce little sexual monster lived inside me. I pictured him as small enough to easily fit in a regular trashcan, but at the same time incredibly powerful. I saw him as a mangy little creature, like Gollum from *The Lord of the Rings,* with hypnotic little beady eyes and razor-sharp claws and fangs. Somehow this little beast had taken up residence in my life, and there wasn't a time during my first 40 years that I lived without him. When I became a Christian at the age of 16, the Tasmanian Devil, as I later named him, did not leave my company. In a mystery, it's as if he somehow had the authority to co-exist with me, and despite my best efforts to evade him, most of the time I was powerless whenever he showed up, which was quite frequently. In our conflict I normally found the strength to hold him off for short periods of time. When he would first come against me, I could restrain him by forcing him into a nearby trashcan, putting the lid on it, and then sitting on top of it using my weight and determination in the attempt to keep him caged. It was me against him. But he was very strong, and he would continuously bang, kick, and claw in rebellion to the internment I had required of him. Inevitably my strength would quickly fade, and despite my valiant effort against him, he would burst out of my fragile confine, leap on top of me, and sink his fangs and claws deep into my flesh — defeating me once again. It's as if he was a cruel dictator, and whenever he commanded my allegiance, I had no choice but to submit to him. I wondered who this Tasmanian Devil was, how he had attached himself to me, and how I could neutralize his presence in my life.

Me, Myself & I

Of course, it wasn't really me against him, as if there were independent personalities involved in this struggle. The Bible does not teach that we are spiritually schizophrenic with three different entities — our old nature, our new nature, and us — living in us. Rather, we are individuals who, as Christians, are free moral agents with the capacity to do either right or wrong.

It should be noted that Christian scholars disagree regarding why Christians continue to sin after salvation. There are various theologies expressed concerning the old nature, the new nature, the flesh, and the human heart. Some suggest the human heart is the real source of the problem and say the heart remains evil even after salvation. They might quote Jeremiah 17:9 to make their point: "The heart is deceitful above all things and beyond cure. Who can understand it?" Others suggest the human heart is not the problem because it becomes good after salvation, and might quote Ezekiel 36:26 as their proof text: "I will give you a new heart and put a new spirit in you; I will remove from you your heart of stone and give you a heart of flesh." Some suggest the source of the problem is not the human heart at all, but the old, or sinful, nature. Others suggest that a Christian does not have an old nature at all, because it was eradicated at the moment of salvation. They might quote II Corinthians 5:17 to make their point, which says, "Therefore, if anyone is in Christ, he is a new creation; the old has gone, the new has come!"

Confused? Well, I'm sorry because it is not my intention to confuse you. My point is simply this: regardless of what you call it, how you explain it, or what your theology is, the fact remains that even after salvation there is something that continually compels Christians to sin. In a nutshell, my personal opinion as a non-theologian is that we do not have an old, or sinful nature as Christians. I believe that at the moment of salvation, we become the children of God, and as such we are given a new nature and a new and good heart that is alive to God. Everything in our lives radically changes the instant we become Christians. Before we were saved we were literally dead to God, and we were by nature objects of God's wrath (Ephesians 2:1-3). After salvation we are made alive to God and are destined to fulfill the good works that God prepared in advance for us to do (Ephesians 2:4-10). As children of God, we are not evil. We are good and we are blessed of God. No, the thing that compels us to sin after we become Christians, the Tasmanian Devil if you will, is not in our hearts or in the nature of who we are; it is in our flesh! As we'll see shortly, the Bible clearly indicates that the tendency to sin in the believer's life is produced by the flesh, which sets itself in direct opposition to the Spirit of God.

A Holy Invasion

The picture the Bible paints of our standing with God before salvation is not pretty. It says we were dead in our sins, that we walked in the ways of the devil, and that we were the objects of God's wrath (Ephesians 2:1-4). It says that as unsaved men we did not have the Spirit of God in our lives, and as a result we did not even have the capacity to know or understand the things of God (I Corinthians 2:14). The alarming passage found in Romans 3:10-18 says, among other things, that we would not seek God, that we had become worthless, that not even one of us would do anything that was good, that our throats were an open grave, that our mouths were full of cursing and bitterness, that ruin and misery marked our ways, and there was no fear of God before our eyes. It's a picture of mankind completely and utterly lost, separated, and alienated from the life of God. It's a picture of sin, hopelessness, and unimaginable darkness.

The Bible then reveals the glory of what happens to us at the very moment of our salvation, when our lives are radically changed by a holy invasion. In an instant, the very moment we believe in Jesus as our Savior, the Holy Spirit of God literally invades our life as He comes to indwell our hearts forever. In this holy invasion the Spirit of God enters our lives, and in a brilliant explosion the light of Christ floods our hearts and forever dispels the darkness that had alienated us from God. The entrance of the Spirit of God into our lives is of monumental significance, and the Bible has much to say about it.

During His last few days before the crucifixion, Jesus told the disciples it was good that He was going away from them, because if He did not leave them, the Holy Spirit would not come to them (John 16:7). After His resurrection and immediately before His ascension into heaven, Jesus told the disciples to wait in Jerusalem for the gift of the Holy Spirit, who would empower them to serve God (Acts 1:4-8). Then, on the day of Pentecost, the Church began when the Holy Spirit fell in power and indwelt the very first believers (Acts 2:1-4). On that day, at the moment of their salvation, the physical bodies of every believer in Christ became the very temples of the Holy Spirit (I Corinthians 6:19). And the same is true for every believer since that day. The Bible also reveals much about the presence and ministry of the Holy Spirit in the lives of believers. It says, among many other things, that if we do not have the Spirit of God in our lives, we do not belong to Christ (Romans 8:9); that we are baptized into the Body of Christ by the Holy Spirit (I Corinthians 12:13); that we are sealed with the Holy Spirit, which guarantees our redemption (Ephesians 1:13-14); and that the Holy Spirit enables us to crucify our sinful passions and live a life that is pleasing and honoring to God (Galatians 5:22-24). It is this invasion of the Holy Spirit into our lives that not only makes us alive to God and empowers us to live the Christian life, but also creates such conflict with our sinful flesh.

Flesh vs. Spirit

The scripture clearly indicates that there is an ongoing conflict between every believer's natural flesh and the Spirit of God.

> This I say then, walk in the Spirit, and ye shall not fulfill the lust of the flesh. For the flesh lusteth against the Spirit, and the Spirit against the flesh; and these are contrary the one to the other, so that ye cannot do the things that ye would. Now the works of the flesh are manifest, which are these: adultery, fornication, uncleanness, lasciviousness, idolatry, sorcery, hatred, strife, jealousy, wrath, factions, seditions, heresies, envyings, murders, drunkenness, revelings, and the like; of which I told you before, as I have also told you in time past, that they who do such things shall not inherit the kingdom of God. But the fruit of the Spirit is love, joy, peace, long-suffering, gentleness, goodness, faith, meekness, and self-control; against such there is no law. And they that are Christ's have crucified the flesh with the affections and lusts. If we live in the Spirit, let us also walk in the Spirit. Galatians 5:17-25, KJV

> For the law of the Spirit of life in Christ Jesus hath made me free from the law of sin and death. For what the law could not do, in that it was weak through the flesh, God sending his own Son, in the likeness of sinful flesh and for sin, condemned sin in the flesh, that the righteousness of the law might be fulfilled in us, who walk not after the flesh, but

after the Spirit…Therefore, brethren, we are debtors, not to
the flesh, to live after the flesh. For if ye live after the flesh,
ye shall die; but if ye, through the Spirit, do mortify the
deeds of the body, ye shall live. Romans 8:2-4, 12-13, KJV

In the past, before you became a Christian, the flesh basically could do
whatever it wanted to do, whenever it wanted. It had no one to answer to
and no one resisting its natural control in your life. But all that changed the
moment you became a Christian. The moment you believed in Jesus as your
personal Savior, the Spirit of God made your life His home, taking up residence in your physical body. At that moment, the flesh and the Spirit were
set in direct opposition to one another, each vying for control of your life.
The flesh is bound to the law of sin and forever pulls you toward sinful patterns and tendencies. The Spirit is bound to the life of God, and continually seeks to bring your life into higher places of submission and obedience
that are pleasing to God. The nature of this ongoing conflict between the
flesh and the Spirit in the life of the believer is important to understand.

Principles of the Flesh

The following five principles help us understand more about the flesh and
how to render it powerless in our lives.

1. When you become a Christian your flesh does not leave you.

Some Christians teach the eradication of the flesh, meaning that the
flesh is somehow done away with or destroyed at salvation. This simply is
not true. Again, whether you call it the flesh, the old nature, the old man,
the lower nature, or the sinful nature, there clearly remains within the lives
of Christians something that compels us to sin and disobey God. Many verses in the Bible reveal that it is possible for Christians to still sin. In I John
1:9 we are told to confess our sin in order to walk in fellowship with God.
Why would we be told to confess our sin if we were not capable of sin to
begin with? In I Corinthians 6:18 we are exhorted to flee from sexual sin.
Why would we be exhorted to flee if we were incapable of sinning? In I
Corinthians 5:1 some of the Corinthian believers had fallen into sexual sin
that most unbelievers would not even commit. Clearly the flesh is still alive
in the Christian's life, and it is possible for Christians to sin.

2. When you become a Christian your flesh does not change.

In John 3:6 Jesus said, "That which is born of the flesh is flesh; and that which is born of the Spirit is spirit." In other words, flesh remains flesh, the flesh never changes, and the flesh is no different after you become a Christian. In Galatians 5:19-21 Paul is writing to Christians and he enumerates the deeds of the flesh. A Christian can commit adultery just like a non-Christian. A Christian can be full of bitterness just like a non-Christian. A Christian can get drunk or commit murder just like a non-Christian. The flesh in a Christian is no different than the flesh in a non-Christian, and the flesh is just as capable of producing its ugly fruit in either one.

3. Christianity is not trying to make your flesh better.

In Galatians 5:24 Paul says, "They that are Christ's have crucified the flesh with the affections and lusts." In other words, we are not called to make our flesh better. We are called to put the deeds of the flesh to death by the power of the Spirit who indwells us. Remember the illustration of the pig? The farmer took the pig out of the barnyard and tried to clean him up. He bathed, perfumed, and dressed up the pig. But as soon as he put the pig back in the barnyard, it ran and jumped right back in the mud. Why? Because you cannot change the nature of a pig, and that which is born a pig will always remain a pig. The flesh is exactly the same. Christianity is not trying to clean up the flesh. Christianity is rendering the flesh powerless by yielding to the power of the indwelling Holy Spirit.

4. There is a conflict between the flesh and the Holy Spirit in the life of every believer.

In Galatians 5:17 Paul graphically portrays the conflict between the flesh and the Spirit. In the original language this verse reads,

> For the flesh constantly has a strong desire to suppress the Spirit, and the Spirit constantly has a strong desire to suppress the flesh. These are entrenched in an attitude of mutual opposition to one another, so that you may not do the things that you desire to do.

In Romans 7:15-25 Paul graphically illustrates further the intense conflict between the flesh and the Spirit as they each vie for control of the Christian's life.

I do not understand what I do. For what I want to do I do not do, but what I hate I do. And if I do what I do not want to do, I agree that the law is good. As it is, it is no longer I myself who do it, but it is sin living in me. I know that nothing good lives in me, that is, in my sinful nature. For I have the desire to do what is good, but I cannot carry it out...

5.   The key to victory over the flesh is yielding to the Holy Spirit.

In Romans 6:16 Paul says, "Know ye not that to whom ye yield yourselves servants to obey, his servants ye are whom ye obey, whether of sin unto death, or of obedience unto righteousness?" In verse 19 of the same passage, Paul goes on to say that just as we used to yield our physical bodies to the flesh, which produced the fruit of sin in our lives, we should now yield our physical bodies to righteousness and holiness. In Galatians 5:16 Paul states how to render the Tasmanian Devil of the flesh powerless in our lives: "This I say then, walk in the Spirit, and ye shall not fulfill the lust of the flesh."

Spiritual Aerodynamics

When a pilot attempts to fly an airplane, there is one major problem: gravity. If the law of gravity had a voice, it would say to the airplane, "You can't get up in the air and fly. You have to stay here on the ground." There is however another law that comes into effect as the airplane begins to speed down the runway: the law of aerodynamics. If the law of aerodynamics had a voice, it would say to the airplane, "You can get up in the air and fly. You don't have to stay here on the ground." As the airplane continues to speed down the runway, a real battle begins to take place. The law of gravity is fighting to hold the airplane on the ground, and the law of aerodynamics is fighting to pull it up in the air. The two contradictory forces are in direct opposition to one another, and for several extended moments a very real conflict rages as each fights for control of the airplane. Then, suddenly, almost magically, the airplane breaks free from the ground and begins soaring into the sky. Why? Because when the law of aerodynamics goes into effect, the law of gravity is rendered powerless! Aerodynamics always wins, because it is a higher law, and when it operates, the law of gravity is overcome. Of course, this does not mean that the law of gravity has disappeared. It still exists, and if the airplane tried to stop in midair it would fall immediately and disastrously to the ground. The law of gravity is always ready and waiting to take over should the law of aerodynamics stop functioning. But as long as the plane is operating according to the law of aerodynamics, it will soar effortlessly over the law of gravity.

In much the same way, the Bible says in Romans 8:2, "Through Christ Jesus the law of the Spirit of life set me free from the law of sin and death." Further, in Galatians 5:16 we are told, "So I say, live by the Spirit, and you will not gratify the desires of the sinful nature." In the same way the law of gravity is rendered powerless by the law of aerodynamics, the flesh is rendered powerless in the life of the believer through the power of the Holy Spirit. Praise God! The flesh is like "spiritual gravity" fighting to hold us down in places of bondage and our old sinful patterns, but the Spirit of God is like "spiritual aerodynamics," which empowers us to soar high above the flesh, the world, and the devil! As we yield to the indwelling Holy Spirit and submit to His power and guidance in our lives, the flesh is rendered powerless and we will be set free to move into higher levels of victory. We need to live our lives according to the law of spiritual aerodynamics!

You are invited to pray the following prayer as you seek to yield your life to the Holy Spirit and experience His power.

A Prayer for Yieldedness to the Holy Spirit

Dear Heavenly Father, I come before you now in the Name of Jesus, and I pray you would cover my entire life with the blood of Christ. I know that as long as I live in my physical body, I will have to contend with the desires of my sinful flesh, and that my flesh is no different today than it was before I was a Christian. I confess to you, oh God, that I have sinned in the past by obeying the passions of my sinful flesh, but from this day forward I pray you would fill me with the Holy Spirit and help me to crucify my flesh. I thank you and praise you for the gift of the Holy Spirit. I thank you that my body is the temple of the Holy Spirit and that He lives within me. I thank you according to your Word that I am sealed with the Holy Spirit and that He can empower me to serve you, oh God, and live a life that is holy and pleasing in your sight. I recognize that there is an ongoing conflict in my life between the flesh and the Spirit, and that the key to victory in this conflict is yielding to the power of the Holy Spirit. I pray, oh God, that you would help me to be controlled by the Holy Spirit, and that the Holy Spirit would not be grieved in my life because of the presence of sin. I thank you that as I yield to the indwelling Holy Spirit, that my flesh is rendered powerless in the same way the law of gravity is rendered powerless by the law of aerodynamics. I say by faith that the law of the Spirit of life has set me free from the law of sin and death. I pray you would help me to grow in the power of the Spirit, that you would convict me of any sin or disobedience in my life, and that you, through the power of the Spirit, would put to death the deeds of my sinful flesh. In the Name of Jesus I speak by faith the following scriptures over my life:

> This I say then, walk in the Spirit, and ye shall not fulfill the lust of the flesh. But the fruit of the Spirit is love, joy, peace, patience, kindness, goodness, faithfulness, gentleness and self-control. Those who belong to Christ Jesus have crucified the sinful nature with its passions and desires. Since we live with the Spirit, let us keep in step with the Spirit. Galatians 5:16-25

> For the law of the Spirit of life in Christ Jesus hath made me free from the law of sin and death. For what the law could not do, in that it was weak through the flesh, God sending his own Son, in the likeness of sinful flesh and for sin, condemned sin in the flesh, that the righteousness of the law might be fulfilled in us, who walk not after the flesh, but after the Spirit… Therefore, brethren, we are debtors, not to the flesh, to live after the flesh. For if ye live after the flesh, ye shall die; but if ye, through the Spirit, do mortify the deeds of the body, ye shall live. Romans 8:2-4, 12-13

I love you, oh God, and I pray all these things in the Name of Jesus Christ my Lord.

Feel free to add any words or prayers from your heart to God.

CHAPTER 9

SEXUAL IDOLATRY

A Jealous God

God is a jealous God, and He will not share His glory with anything or anyone else (Exodus 33:14). I am not a theologian, but I believe this is the primary theme of the entire Bible. In fact, the Bible is really the story of how God is bringing all things in heaven and earth full circle back into submission to His absolute divine authority. You see, in eternity past, God was God! He was the one and only absolute divine authority in heaven. He alone was the object of all praise, honor, and glory. He was God, and all creatures and all things were in complete submission to His divine rule and will. He alone was the center of heaven. He alone was the object of all worship. He alone was respected and honored as the only supreme and almighty God. All creatures in heaven recognized, respected, and submitted to God's supreme authority. His position as God was undisputed. His glory as God was undisputed. He alone was recognized as the exalted, holy, high and lifted up, awesome, and all-powerful God. That is, until one day when a seed of rebellion was born, and there was mutiny against the throne of God for the first time.

Mutiny in Heaven

Don't ask me how or why it happened, but somehow pride was born in the heart of Lucifer, a mighty and beautiful angel, and he determined in his heart that he would rise up in rebellion against God, overthrow the throne of God, and assume for himself the very position of God (Isaiah 14:12-17). In a further mystery, he was somehow able to persuade one-third of the angels in heaven to enlist in his rebellious sedition (Revelation 12:4), and after they failed to overthrow the throne of God through force, they were vomited from heaven and cast to the earth until the end of time (Revelation 12:7-9).

For the first time, living creatures existed in autonomy and rebellion against God. There were creatures that no longer recognized God as the supreme authority of heaven and earth. They refused to submit to God's rule and will alone and rejected God as the sole object of all praise, honor, glory, and worship. A kind of grand cosmic conflict was born in the universe: the Kingdom of God against the kingdom of Satan. The combatants were fighting for ultimate control of heaven, and their conflict was advanced to the center stage of planet Earth.

Mutiny in the Garden

Some time after Satan was rejected from heaven, God created Adam and Eve. The Bible clearly teaches that, among other reasons, God created mankind to love us and wanted to be in relationship with us. The Bible says that God walked with Adam and Eve in the cool of the day (Genesis 3:8). It goes on to reveal that God loves us (Ephesians 3:17-19); that we are His children (John 1:12); that we are His friends (John 15:15); and that He has given us everything we need for life and godliness (II Peter 1:3). Surely if we even began to write about them, God's promises and provisions for us would require multiple volumes of books, and the angels themselves long to understand the depth of God's grace toward those made in the very image of God (I Peter 1:12).

In view of this special place Adam and Eve held in God's heart, it didn't take Satan long to devise a new plan to attack the heart and Kingdom of God. Since his plan to overthrow the throne of God through brute force already failed, he determined to assault the throne of God by switching to "Plan B." He thought, "I will harm the heart and kingdom of God by attacking and destroying what God loves so much: I will harm mankind. I will mar those made in the image of God. I will incite autonomy and rebellion in them against God, and then God will be forced to kick them out of heaven, the same way He kicked me out of heaven. I will ruin the beauty of God's image-bearers; I will forever separate God from His beloved; and in so doing I will bring harm to the throne of God." In a mystery, God's creation of man became the central stage on which the cosmic conflict between good and evil would play itself out.

Almost immediately after creation, the evil one deceived Adam and Eve into disobeying the direct command and will of God. God had very clearly instructed Adam not to eat of the tree of the knowledge of good and evil, yet Adam and Eve both quickly chose to disobey God when confronted with the devil's crafty handiwork. It seems that Satan easily deceived mankind into the same posture of autonomy, rebellion, and disobedience that lived in his own heart. Now, not only was there rebellion and mutiny in heaven, but there was also rebellion and mutiny on earth.

This moment — the moment of mankind's disobedience to God — was a monumental moment in all of eternity, and we should be careful not to rush by it too quickly. In fact, if we could truly comprehend all that happened in this single moment, we would surely shutter with horror. This was far from a simple mistake that Adam and Eve had made. It was not a mistake that could be easily cleaned up in a moment and then forgotten about in the next.

Instead, the reality of what happened in this moment and the resulting consequences are far more terrible and profound than one could ever communicate with mere words. When Adam and Eve chose to disobey God, it was not a simple mistake. It was an outright and deliberate act of disobedience, defiance, autonomy, insolence, insubordination, rebellion, disrespect, contempt, disdain, disregard, hatred, and mutiny. It was mankind defiantly shaking his fist in the very face of God. It was the equivalent of mankind spitting in the face of God. It was mankind giving God the "finger." It was mankind saying to God through his actions. "You are not God. You do not know what is best. You are not the supreme God of heaven and earth who deserves to be honored and obeyed. Your way is not the only way. We do not have to submit to you, obey you, or listen to what you say. We can do whatever we want. We know what is best for our lives. We are capable of making our own decisions and managing our own lives. We do not have to submit to your rule and your will for our lives. We will determine our own future and destiny without you."

By inciting this horrible rebellion in man, Satan dealt a serious blow to the heel of God (Genesis 3:15), and God was now confronted with even more rebellion among His created beings. As a result, God banished mankind from His presence in the same way He had banished Satan from heaven, but unbeknownst to Satan, the battle for the heart and devotion of man had only just begun.

Back to the Garden

Ever since that fateful day in the Garden of Eden, the cosmic conflict has been raging. In a very elementary way, planet Earth is like a giant checkerboard. God is on one side, pursuing the heart of every man, woman, boy, and girl in His attempt to bring every living soul back from the place of autonomous rebellion to the place of intimate fellowship and willing submission to His absolute divine authority (II Peter 3:9). God is seeking to restore mankind back to the garden; back to the place where we can walk with Him in the cool of the day. On the other side of the checkerboard is the devil, attempting to incite in the heart of every living person autonomy and rebellion against God, and in a rage is making war against those who would obey the commands of God (Revelation 12:17). In the middle, acting as the pawns in the game, are you and I, along with every other person who has ever lived on planet Earth, or ever will live. It is a giant, awesome, astonishing cosmic conflict, and the stakes are incredibly high! Satan is fighting to destroy the glory of God by inspiring rebellion against the throne of God, and God is fighting to bring all things in heaven and earth full circle back into submission to his absolute divine authority for his ultimate praise and glory. As mentioned at the very beginning of this chapter, the central theme of the entire Bible is the glory of God. The very cry of God's heart throughout the Bible and throughout the ages has been for a people who will put God back in His rightful place as supreme authority — deserving of all glory, honor, praise, and worship.

God Hates Idolatry

As we begin to comprehend the backdrop of this grand cosmic conflict, it becomes easy to understand why God hates idolatry. He is the only true God worthy of all glory and praise, yet autonomy and rebellion are prevalent among his created beings. Rather than acknowledging and worshipping God as the only true God, worthy of all praise and glory, mankind has instead rejected the true God and has turned to worship and serve a myriad of false gods. That's what idolatry is: when we take the glory, honor, and praise that belongs to God alone and we instead give it to anything or anyone else but God. Idolatry is when we allow something other than God to be the very center and purpose of our lives. Idolatry is when we give our heart, devotion, and passion to something other than God. Idolatry is a direct affront to God, because it is doing to Him exactly what Lucifer did in eternity past, and exactly what Adam and Eve did in the garden. Idolatry is spitting in God's face and giving Him the "finger." Idolatry is saying to God, "You are not my God. You do not know what is best. You are not the supreme God of heaven and earth who deserves to be honored and obeyed. You alone are not worthy to be the object of my heart's attention and affection. I do not choose to make you the center and purpose of my life. I do not want to live for you. I choose to live for, and give my heart to, this other false god." Wow! No wonder God hates idolatry, and no wonder He has so much to say about it.

Note: The topic of idolatry is of such significance in the Bible there is no way to give it justice in the short space of this chapter. I highly recommend, if you want to do an awesome study that will bless your socks off, that you consult your concordance for the many passages in the Bible that use the words *idol, idols, idolater,* and *idolatry.* You will be amazed and blown away by what God has to say about idolatry. For our purpose here, suffice it to say that God hates idolatry, because God hates anything that competes with His rightful place as God in our hearts and lives.

No Other Gods

On Mount Sinai, a short time after He had led the nation of Israel out of Egypt, God gave Moses the Ten Commandments. In these Ten Commandments, God reduced the entire Law and Prophets into ten concise directives that were to govern man's relationship with God and his fellow man. The first four commandments have to do with man's relationship with God, and the last six commandments have to do with man's relationship with man. It only makes sense that these ten directives are of supreme importance to God and represent the central values He expects to govern the lives and relationships of mankind. Although all ten of the commandments are no doubt very important, note what God communicated through the preeminent positions of commandments number one and two. "You shall have no other gods before me. You shall not make for yourself an idol in the form of anything in heaven above or on the earth beneath or in the waters below" (Exodus 20:3-4).

Wow! The first two commandments focus on establishing the preeminent position of God in the heart and life of man. According to *Strong's Concordance,* the word "before" used in the first commandment is a Hebrew word that means "above, over, beside, to ascend, to arise, to exalt, to mount up." In other words God is saying, "You shall have no other gods above me, over me, or beside me. You shall have no other gods that attempt to ascend, rise up, mount up, or exalt themselves above me." Further, God continues in the second commandment that we are to have no idols and specifically mentions three places from where we should not make idols in our lives: heaven above, earth beneath, or water below. That pretty much covers everything! In other words, God is saying there is no place man should go to find anything to take the place of God in his life, not in heaven, or on the earth, or under the earth. God alone is to be our God. He alone is to be the supreme object of our attention, affection, desire, purpose, praise, and worship. Our lives are to be in complete submission and surrender to Him as the one and only almighty God. Clearly it is of supreme importance to God that we have no other gods or idols in our lives.

The Pain of Life

The book of Judges contains an interesting story that helps us understand more of the nature of idolatry (Judges 17:1-5). A man named Micah had apparently stolen eleven hundred shekels of silver from his own mother. When Micah realized how upset his mother was that the silver had been taken, he confessed and returned it to her. She was so delighted to have the silver returned, out of appreciation she gave two hundred shekels to a silversmith so he could make an idol for her son to add to the collection of idols he already had. Micah had a shrine in his home, a house of gods, including the following: carved and melted images; an ephod, which was one of the high priest's garments to be worn in the process of worship; and a teraphim, which was another kind of family idol.

According to *Strong's Concordance,* the word "teraphim" in the Hebrew language means "a healer, to mend by stitching the way a physician would heal or repair, to cure and make whole." In other words, a *teraphim* was a false god, an idol, that people turned to in order to seek healing and comfort from life's pain. This idea is substantiated by the context of the passage itself. When Micah's mother lost the silver, it's as if a great pain or sorrow came into her life. As a result of this sense of loss, she was apparently quite upset and even uttered a curse (v. 2). When she was fortunate enough to regain the silver, with a heart of gratitude she had an idol made as her way of giving thanks for her good fortune. Rather than worshipping and giving thanks to the true God, she turned her heart toward an idol that she saw as the healer and provider of her life. How sad. Yet her example gives us insight into the nature of idolatry.

In a mystery, pain has a way of revealing the false gods we tend to serve. We live in a fallen world, and surely there is plenty of pain to go around. Consider where you go for comfort whenever and for whatever reasons pain comes into your life. Who do you turn to for healing? What do you seek in the attempt to soothe your aching heart? What is the first thing you reach for in the effort to anesthetize your soul? The answer to these questions will help you identify the idols you tend to worship. When confronted with a sense of loss and pain in her life, Micah's mother turned to an idol for healing and comfort. A business acquaintance recently confessed to me that after an exceptionally difficult week at work, he felt compelled to go to a bar and drink. After drinking all day he took a cab to a strip club and spent the last of his money one dollar at a time as he watched naked women dance in front of him. Some people turn to chocolate; others turn to food, shopping, television, or work. Some people turn to drugs, while others turn to sports or their favorite pastime. Some people sleep; others use masturbation to relieve themselves, because it allows them to escape the reality of their painful lives, if only for the few minutes of pleasure their false god provides them. When the sting, pain, or disappointment of life pricks our hearts, the voices of a myriad of false gods beckon us with their promises to soothe, comfort, and heal us, and many times we respond to their calls as we rush to the relief they promise (Jeremiah 2:23-25). I wonder where you and I have the tendency to turn in our attempt to soothe and heal our lives?

Sexual Idolatry

Keeping in mind the cosmic conflict and the central importance of the glory of God versus idolatry, we can now turn our attention back to the issue at hand: sexual purity! What does all this have to do with sexual purity, you ask? My response: everything! I propose that one of the most common forms of idolatry in the lives of Christian men is sexual idolatry.

We may not even realize we are doing it, but at times we literally worship the false god of sex. We turn to sex as the *teraphim,* or healer of our lives. We think about, long for, and adore sex; we devote our hearts, time, energy, and passion toward sex. No matter how often we have sex, it is not enough. Not even sex with the beautiful woman God has given us in marriage is enough to satisfy the seemingly insatiable sexual hunger that lives in our soul. We want more than just our wives. We often feed our hungry eyes on the women around us every day, and we fantasize about what it would be like to be with our neighbor's wife. Our lives can become consumed by our desire and drive for sex. Sex becomes central to our lives.

The power this false god wields over us is so significant, that when it calls us to worship we immediately turn our backs on the true God and bow down in reverence to the true emperor in our hearts. Although our minds know we should not engage in the secret activities we delight in, we are powerless to resist because the heart of man will always worship his true god. And so we continue to look at dirty magazines, or sneak on the Internet when no one else is looking. We allow lust to rage in our hearts as the impure thoughts of our minds run rampant. We masturbate endlessly, we call phone numbers we shouldn't, and watch movies we shouldn't. We look at women, think about women, and say things to women that are uncalled for. We may even visit strip clubs, engage the services of prostitutes, or indulge in the false luxury of an adulterous affair. And why do we do these things? Because we worship the false god of our own sexuality!

Fire from Heaven

God is longing to expose the false gods in our lives. He is longing to break the power of every idol in our lives and to turn our hearts toward Him as the one and only true God we love and worship. The question Elijah asked of the people on Mount Carmel is an appropriate question for you and I today. "How long will you waver between two opinions? If the LORD is God, follow him; but if Baal is God, follow him" (1 Kings 18:21). On that glorious day, fire fell from heaven and consumed the false idols and the prophets of Baal. Elijah had prayed, "Answer me, O LORD, answer me, so these people will know that you, O LORD, are God, and that you are turning their hearts back again" (1 Kings 18:37). When the fire of the Lord fell from heaven and consumed His enemies, the people responded accordingly: "When all the people saw this, they fell prostrate and cried, The LORD — He is God! The LORD — He is God!" (1 Kings 18:38-39).

It seems to me that this is exactly what we need in our lives. We need God to turn our hearts back again. We need the Lord to bring the fire of heaven into our lives to destroy every false god and idol. We need Jesus to do for us what we could never do for ourselves. We need Him to break through bars of iron and cut through gates of bronze. We need Him to proclaim freedom over our captivity, release from the darkness of our prisons, and the day of vengeance of our God against every unholy and ungodly influence in our lives. He is the one and only true God. He alone deserves all praise, honor, glory, and worship. We have lived long enough in places of autonomy, rebellion, and disobedience. Now is the time to move back to the Garden. Now is the time to walk with God in the cool of the day.

Are you willing to pray the following prayer from your heart, specifically asking God to break the power of every false god and sexual idolatry from your life?

A Prayer Renouncing Sexual Idolatry

Dear Heavenly Father, I know that you alone are the only true God. There is no other God but you, and you alone deserve all honor, glory, praise, and worship. You alone are the absolute supreme authority of heaven and earth, and you are the almighty God. You are the holy, exalted, high and lifted up, awesome, and all-powerful God. You say in your holy Word that you are a jealous God, and you will not share your glory with any other. Every other god beside you is a false, worthless, powerless, and impotent god. Every other god beside you is deaf, dumb, blind, mute, and lame. You alone are the maker of heaven and earth, and there is no other god, in heaven above, on the earth beneath, or in the water below, that deserves to be acknowledged as god but you.

I know, dear God, that you are the only God I should esteem in my heart and life. You alone deserve to be the object of my devotion, surrender, service, adoration, submission, praise, and worship. I acknowledge that you are the true God, and there should be no other god in my life that competes with your rightful place of supreme authority in my life. I acknowledge your rightful place as the true God of my life, and I completely submit my life to you in every way.

I confess to you, oh God, that I have sinned against you in the past by allowing false gods to rule and reign in my heart. I have loved, served, obeyed, and given my heart and devotion to these false gods, and in so doing I have broken the first two commandments, committing idolatry. I pray, oh God, that you would forgive my idolatry, and forgive me for giving my heart away to lesser gods than you. I ask that you would expose every false god and idol in my heart that competes with your right to the throne of my life. I pray you would help me to see and understand my idolatry so I can cast every idol down and dispose of it like a used menstrual cloth (Isaiah 30:22). I pray you would give me eyes to see and ears to hear whatever you desire to reveal to me, and I pray that you would change my heart. I pray for the gift of repentance, and I pray that you alone would become the exalted and only true God of my heart.

Father in heaven, I specifically confess to you the sin of sexual idolatry, and I pray for your grace and your forgiveness. I confess that I have dishonored you by allowing my sexuality to assume an inappropriate place of power and authority in my life. I specifically confess the following behaviors that reveal the sexual idolatry in my life:

_____

_____

_____

(Specifically name any ways your sexuality has been manifesting itself as an idol in your life. Also, name any other idolatry in your life you are aware of currently.)

Heavenly Father, I confess that when I allow these sinful behaviors in my life, I am serving a false god instead of you, the true God. I pray you would enable me thorough the power of the Holy Spirit to honor you from this day forward with my sexuality, and that my sexuality would be in complete submission to your rule, reign, and authority in my life. In the Name of Jesus I renounce the false god of sexual idolatry in my life. I pray that you would rebuke this false emperor in my life and break any remaining power it holds over me. I pray for the blood of Jesus to completely cover my life and my sexuality, and I pray for purity in my life that would bring honor and glory to you as my true God.

Feel free to add any words or prayers from your heart to God.

PART 3

FORTIFYING INITIATIVES

THE DAWNING OF A NEW DAY

The process of my repentance and redemption was kind of like crossing a creek on a series of stepping-stones. As I began walking the pathway of repentance, God would reveal to me each step of submission He was requiring of me, and as I obeyed Him to the best of my ability, He would bless me accordingly and then reveal the next stepping-stone in the proper time. In this way, the redemption of my life, my sexuality, and my marriage unfolded over a period of time, like the dawning of a new day.

It's as if the sexual area of my life, for a long time, was surrounded by the darkness of a long, cold night. Then slowly, almost imperceptibly at first, I began to discern the very first hint of light coming over the ever-present dark horizon. In time, as the Hound of Heaven continued His relentless pursuit of my heart and life, and as I surrendered to His holy initiatives accordingly, the night sky on the horizon slowly began to come alive and dance with an array of beautiful colors, as blackness gave way to mystical hues of orange, red, and yellow. As my divine aggressor overtook more and more of my heart, the darkness that had always surrounded me seemed to lose its shadowy grip on my life and reluctantly began retreating. Darkness always surrenders to light! As more and more light began surrounding my life, there was less and less darkness, and with the growing light came my ability to see more clearly than ever before. Imagine walking through a field in the pitch dark compared to walking through the same field in the light of day. I began to move about my life in greater levels of freedom and agility than I had ever

123

known before, and the obstacles that used to trip me up because of my inability to recognize them lost their power to impede my progress. I could now clearly see my obstacles and move around and through them accordingly. There was indeed a new day dawning, and the light of Christ was changing everything about my life.

> The path of the righteous is like the first gleam of dawn,
> shining ever brighter till the full light of day. But the way of
> the wicked is like deep darkness; they do not know what
> makes them stumble. Proverbs 4:18-19

I wish I could say God somehow radically changed my life and all of my problems in an instant; that there was one glorious moment where every sin, bondage, and captivity was forever shattered and removed. I have no doubt God could do such a thing if He wanted to, but in my case it was more of a process over a period of time, and is in fact a process I am still walking in.

In this final section, we will consider several of the fortifying initiatives God placed along my pathway of sexual repentance and redemption. Some of them may apply to your life and others may not. As you reflect upon them, may God speak deeply into your heart as He invites you to continue along the pathway of repentance He has designed for your life.

CHAPTER 10

A Holy Altar, Sacrifice, & Vow

An Unholy Coalition

In my life, for years the power of my sinful flesh, like spiritual gravity, held me captive in ongoing places of bondage, defeat, and sinful patterns. It's as if there was an unholy coalition aligned against me. This coalition was comprised not only of my flesh, but was reinforced by many of the chains of bondage we have already discussed, including the following: the root of pornography, the power of ungodly role models, generational sin, sexual abuse, and spiritual idolatry. The power of any one of these dark forces in my life alone would have been strong enough, but as they united in their unholy alliance, their power exponentially increased, and their collective strength against my sexuality was substantially greater than the power they could have exerted individually. No wonder I found myself in such terrible sexual bondage, unable to honor God or my wife with my sexuality. The enemy very effectively took me out of the battle and rendered my Christian life essentially powerless as he, with precision accuracy, entangled me in the web of sexual bondage; a web that consisted of the various strands mentioned above. I had fallen overboard; I desperately needed a savior. Through the ruin of my sexuality, the enemy was bringing maximum destruction to bear in my life as he attempted to destroy everything of significance to me. That is, until God engineered a process of events that would break the unholy power of my flesh, shattering the unholy chains that had held me captive for so long.

Glorious Ruin

In the unexpected way God can bring life out of death through the mystery of the gospel, God began interrupting my life during my darkest and most painful days. These days were dark because of my involvement in an ongoing affair with the wife of my friend, and they were painful because of the disastrous reality of my own marriage. Through a series of events far too complicated to convey in the short space of this chapter, God in His sovereignty began to disrupt the path of destruction on which my life was proceeding, in much the same way the angel of the Lord hindered the path on which the foolish prophet Balaam and his donkey were traveling (Numbers 22:21-32). (For details of these events in my life, read chapters 18-21 in *Stories*.) It was through the application of what I now call God's "heavy hand" (Psalm 32:4-5) that He mysteriously brought me to a place of deeper brokenness before Him than I had ever experienced before. I was 37 years old at the time, and after struggling and failing so deeply with my sexuality for 37 years, God finally brought me to a place of glorious ruin.

For my entire Christian life I had tried, and failed, to manage my sexuality through an endless series of tips and techniques, self-efforts, and self-determinations. I was like a farmer who for 37 years tried to clean up the pig in his barnyard, and after 37 years I finally realized that no matter how hard I tried I would never be able to control my sexuality in a way that would honor God. Like the first rays of brilliant light exploding over the horizon at sunrise after a long night of seemingly endless storms, the realization of my total and utter inability to ever change myself mysteriously brought with it the hope of a new and glorious day. With more depth and clarity than I had ever known before, I realized through the wonderful ministry of God's heavy hand that I was a man who had fallen overboard. I finally saw with clarity that no matter how hard I tried I would never be able to change my life or my sexuality through the power of my own self-effort or initiative. With a shudder of horror it's as if God allowed me to see, not intellectually from my head but realistically from my heart, just how lost and desperate I really was without Him. This realization was so completely overwhelming that it caused me to cry out to God from a more broken and desperate heart than I had ever known. After 37 years of sin, failure, self-effort, and unimaginable pain, God had finally brought me to a place of glorious ruin, which mysteriously became the gateway to my repentance and healing.

What is Repentance?

I began groping my way along the mysterious and unfamiliar pathway of repentance God had so graciously required of me; a pathway that included, among other things: confession of sin, submission to authority, attending professional counseling, and joining a small group of men who were fellow strugglers. (For details of these events in my life read chapters 22-25 in *Stories.*) It was during the early months of this new and redemptive journey in my life that God engineered a series of events that eventually broke the power of my sinful flesh and shattered the chains of bondage that had held me captive for so long.

As I met weekly with my therapist we discussed the idea of biblical repentance. As we pondered this topic one day, my therapist recommended I talk with several loved and respected Christian friends of mine regarding their thoughts and feedback concerning repentance. I liked his idea, so I created a "repentance survey" that consisted of five questions and I determined to interview several Christian friends accordingly. The five questions on my survey were:

1. What is repentance?
2. Why is repentance important in the life of a Christian?
3. What should a Christian do in order to experience true repentance?
4. How does a Christian know if he has experienced true repentance?
5. What other thoughts or comments do you have on this subject?

Over the next 5 weeks, I interviewed a total of nine different Christian friends, including several pastors, and although each interview was interesting and helpful, one particular meeting became what I later called a "divine appointment."

A Divine Appointment

This particular meeting was with the pastor of a large and well-known church in the St. Louis area, and although I did not know him very well personally, I did respect him from a distance and thought he would be a good person to talk with. As we sat down for lunch one day, we began our discussion and I introduced my questionnaire. I explained to him that I was in therapy dealing with my marriage and other issues, and as part of my process I was interviewing respected Christian friends on the topic of repentance. He immediately responded by telling me he would be glad to answer my questions to the best of his ability, but he inquired further and wondered if I would be willing to share with him what was really going on in my life and what was really behind the purpose of the survey. I therefore proceeded to share my story with him, and as he listened intently, I disclosed to him an overview of my life, my marriage, and my sexuality. I didn't hide anything from him, and I confessed to him the details of my deep battle with my sexuality for so many years, the depth of my moral failure, and the struggle of my difficult marriage.

As he listened carefully to my story, he interrupted me at one point near the end and said he had a question for me about masturbation. "Tony, I know you have struggled with masturbation in your past, but how are you doing with it now? Are you continuing to masturbate at this time in your life?" I responded by confessing, with a sense of embarrassment and shame, that I was continuing to masturbate, but I really didn't see any alternative because of the difficulties in my marriage. I explained that my wife was unwilling to have sex with me for prolonged periods that usually consisted of many months at a time, and I figured masturbating was at least better than committing adultery. As he inquired further about my practice of masturbation, I shared with him about my lifelong struggle with the issue. I told him about finding my father's pornography when I was a boy and how I started masturbating at a very young age. As he listened carefully to my story, he said he wanted to challenge me regarding this issue in my life and wanted to share some things with me.

He then shared what he believed was God's design and purpose for the expression of sexuality within the God-ordained parameters of marriage. He said he believed the Bible teaches that we are to honor God and honor our wives with our sexuality. He said that my sexuality is really a God-given gift exclusively to my wife through the vessel of my body, and that likewise, her sexuality is a God-given gift exclusively to me through the vessel of her body. He said that my wife is the only one who has the right to my sexuality, because it is a gift for her that God has placed within the vessel of my body. He said my sexuality belongs to her and to no one else, and to express my sexuality apart from her would be wrong because that is not how God intends for my sexuality to be expressed. Thus, he said it would be wrong in God's eyes for me to ever express my sexuality in any way apart from my wife, including looking at pornography, having an affair, or even masturbating. These things would be wrong he said, because in such instances I would be opening the gift of my sexuality for my own pleasure, apart from my wife and the God-designed purpose of how my sexuality is to be used.

As my pastor friend shared these thoughts, I saw in my mind's eye a Christmas gift. I realized, that based upon what he was saying, that using my sexuality without my wife is like secretly opening and using someone else's Christmas gift, when in fact it doesn't even belong to me. He then asked me to consider his thoughts, and asked if I would be willing to pray about completely surrendering my body, my sexuality, and my penis to God in a new way. He asked me if I would consider making a vow to honor both God and my wife with my sexuality, which would mean I could never again express my sexuality (including masturbation) apart from my wife.

I had never heard such an idea in my life, and although something deep in my heart was wooed by the poetry of his thoughts and words, I immediately objected and told him I thought such a standard would be impractical for me to maintain, especially given the impossible circumstances of my marriage. I pleaded, "Pastor, you don't understand what my life is like! My wife won't have sex with me! Months pass and I am not allowed to touch her. If I surrendered my sexuality to my wife alone, then my sexuality would never be expressed because she almost never wants it. What will I do? How can I possibly die so completely to myself to make such a thing possible?" Despite my desperate questions and my obvious sense of being so completely overwhelmed by what he was saying, my Christian friend was unyielding in the strength of what he was calling me to do, and he answered me without apology.

"Tony, you can't do it! In fact, it will be impossible for you to do, and that's why you will have to cast yourself so completely on God's grace and depend on Him more desperately every day than you ever have in your entire life. You will need His help and His mercy, every day, every hour, every moment! If He does not help you, then you will not be helped. But I believe that if you make this decision, and if you surrender your sexuality to God from a broken and desperate heart, that He will keep His end of the bargain. I'm not saying it will be easy, but He is a big God, and He can give you victory!"

Hot Deserts & Cool Water

As we continued to talk, the Holy Spirit began to show my heart another kind of vision, and although I did not share it with my pastor friend, I sensed in my heart it was a kind of strange gift from God. As my pastor friend was talking, I saw myself in a vast and hot desert. In this vision I was single. I realized God was calling me to a journey, and as I was about to begin my journey, God placed around my neck a vessel of cool and clean water. I realized I would need this life-giving provision of water to sustain me as I faced the difficult journey ahead, but then I heard the voice of God instructing me. He told me that the vessel of water was not for me. He told me it was His provision for someone else — someone I was going to find along my journey: the person who would become my wife. He said He saw this beauty in the desert, that He was sending me to rescue her, and that she would be thirsty when I found her. He said He trusted me with the stewardship of delivering to her the cool water I carried around my neck.

When I realized I could not drink from the canteen God had placed around my neck, I objected and reminded God that the journey would be long and the desert was very hot. "But God, I will need water to drink. What will I do? How can I make this journey?" He answered me and said that when I found her, she would also be carrying a vessel of water, and that vessel would have my name written on it. He said that we would be very thirsty along the journey, but He wanted us to wait for one another to drink. He promised that when we found one another we could drink deeply from the vessel we each provided for one another, and He was trusting us to wait for one another.

As the meaning of this beautiful vision crossed the threshold of my understanding, my heart began to break as I realized how deeply I had failed in the stewardship God had entrusted to me. I knew that I had started my journey long ago, and that all along the way I had failed to protect the vessel God had placed around my neck: the vessel of my sexuality, which God intended as a gift for me to deliver to my wife. Rather than protecting this precious vessel and saving it for the one to whom it belonged, I opened it early in my journey, gave it away to others, and spilled it all along the ground. I realized how deeply I had failed God and how deeply I had failed my wife. Tears began streaming down my face as I realized my failure, and I felt overwhelmed with a sense of loss because of what I had done.

But then, in a mystery, I sensed the presence of God inviting me through the words of my Christian friend. He told me that God is the God of grace and the God of second chances. I sensed that God was inviting me to a new beginning, and He was willing to place a new vessel around my neck, with a fresh supply of cool and clean water. I sensed that the place I was standing was somehow a holy place, and that mystically this had become a powerful and holy moment in my life. Like Moses at the burning bush, I heard the voice of God calling me through a holy fire, but like Moses, I felt overwhelmed that I could not do what God was asking me to do. I asked my friend if he would pray over me, and as he began to pray my heart seemed to break deeper than ever before. With my usually stiff neck broken in sorrow, I bowed my head in submission to God to match the stature of my broken heart, and I symbolically took off my shoes in reverence of the holy ground on which I was standing.

A Holy Altar, Sacrifice, and Vow

As the pastor finished his prayer, he told me he would be a witness of my vow before God if I were ready to make such a commitment. He said I should see a kind of altar in my mind's eye and that I should lay my body, my sexuality, and my penis on the altar of sacrifice to God. I sensed I was in the very presence of God, and I clearly understood what he was asking of me. I began to pray through my tears, and I cried out for God to save me. I began confessing my sin and my failure to God, and I told God that I wanted to do what I had never done in my entire life. I told Him I wanted to honor Him and honor my wife with my sexuality. I told Him I was sick and tired of my sin and my failure and my pain. I told Him I wanted to do the right thing and surrender my sexuality and my body to Him. I told Him I wanted to save myself for my wife and never wanted to express my sexuality apart from her again. But even as I prayed, my heart broke even deeper because I knew the complete impossibility of my pledge. My heart groaned as I cried out in desperation, because I knew I could not do such a thing.

I told God I wanted to make this vow, but I was afraid that I would fail. I knew in my heart that I had made so many promises to God in the past and had failed repeatedly. I did not want to make another vain promise, and I begged Him to do for me what I could not do for myself, pleading for His mercy and grace. I pictured in my mind an altar of sacrifice, and I pictured myself placing my body, my sexuality, and my penis on the altar. As I did this, I knew these things that had been so much the center of my life for so long no longer belonged to me; they belonged to God, and I would have to trust Him completely. In that moment I surrendered these parts of my life to Him, and I promised God that I would honor Him and my wife from that moment on, by His grace, to the best of my ability. On the pathway of repentance I was traveling, God brought me to this significant moment of glorious defeat, and it was only later I recognized this event as one of the most important and sacred of my life.

The Swimming Pool & A Taste of Freedom

Many months had passed since the day I made my vow, and although nothing seemed to be changing outwardly in the circumstances of my marriage, something happened one day that revealed my first taste of true freedom from my sexual bondage. It proved that God was slowly, almost imperceptibly, changing something inside of me. One day, my boys wanted me to take them to the neighborhood public swimming pool. After arriving at the pool, I sat on a lounge chair on the pool deck and passed the time reading a book and enjoying the sunshine as my boys played nearby in the water. I occasionally looked up to watch my boys splash and romp, and as I looked up one time, I quickly noticed right in front of me a beautiful girl wearing a skimpy bikini. I couldn't help but notice her, and as I began to follow her with my eyes, I quickly caught myself, realized what I was doing, and brought my eyes back to the book I had been reading. I thought to myself, "That's the last thing I need to be looking at!"

I continued to read when suddenly something occurred to me: I was at a swimming pool and there were girls in bikinis everywhere. I looked up, and as I looked all around me, I realized I was surrounded by bikinis and flesh! There were numerous girls all around me at the pool, and most of them were wearing the kind of swimming suits that would be hard not to notice. The startling realization occurred to me that I was surrounded by all these beautiful girls in skimpy bikinis, and I had not even noticed!

As these thoughts flooded me and I tried to understand their meaning, something happened to me that had never happened before, and that is very hard to describe: I felt the Holy Spirit leap for joy within me, and it was only later I imagined it must have been the same way the Holy Spirit caused the baby in Elizabeth's womb to leap when Mary visited her (Luke 1:39-41). I couldn't believe I had been in that environment, surrounded by bikinis, and I hadn't even noticed all those beautiful and scantily clad girls. With a sense of unbelief I realized this was a significant and holy event for me, and with tears streaming down my face I basked in the warm glow of my first taste of freedom and victory over the sexual bondage that had held me captive for so long. In that precious moment it's as if I could hear angels in heaven and the voice of God rejoicing over me, "See Tony! I am God! I am giving you the victory! I am doing for you what you could never do for yourself! I am setting you free! I am breaking the chains. I am making you a new man and I am giving you a new heart!" It was one of the most powerful and glorious moments of my life.

> I will go before you and will level the mountains; I will break down gates of bronze and cut through bars of iron. I will give you the treasures of darkness, riches stored in secret places, so that you may know that I am the LORD, the God of Israel, who summons you by name. Isaiah 45:2-3

Broken Flesh & Severed Roots

As I groped along the pathway of my repentance and followed God in submission to the vow He required of me, He blessed my obedience by breaking the power my flesh had always held over me in the sexual area of my life. He then subsequently began to sever the various roots of bondage that had been holding me captive. One by one, God brought me to places of deeper understanding and repentance concerning these various roots, including the six we have already discussed: pornography, ungodly role models, generational sin, sexual abuse, the flesh, and sexual idolatry. As I understood the power of these various evil influences in my life, I learned to seek God, to repent, and to weep over each one of them. It was through this continued process of repentance that God radically began to change my life, my sexuality, and my marriage.

In Ephesians 1:19-20 Paul says that the same incomparably great power that God used to raise Jesus from the dead is the very power God uses in the lives of those who believe. Glory to God! God had raised Jesus from the dead, and with the same power He was now bringing my sexuality from places of death and bondage to places of life and freedom! Although the redemption of my life has continued to unfold as a process over a period of time (see chapters 27-35 in *Stories*), God has slowly and faithfully worked in my life, my sexuality, my wife's life, and our marriage as healing, restoration, and blessing have been unleashed in greater measures in our lives. This is a process that will no doubt continue until the day we go to heaven (Philippians 1:6), but at this writing, because of God's love, grace, mercy, power, and faithfulness, I am happy to report that I have honored my vow for over 4 years by not expressing my sexuality apart from my wife's involvement or knowledge! Because of Jesus, the one who promised in Isaiah 61 that He can bind up the brokenhearted, bring freedom to captives, and release for those in the darkness of prison, I have been empowered to do something for the past 4 years of my life that I was incapable of doing for the first 40 years of my life. I am bringing maximum glory to God through the very area of my life the evil one attempted to destroy me with, and as a result I am bringing maximum insult to the devil! Glory to God!

What Would God Ask of You?

In chapter 1 I posed the following question:

What would it mean for you to honor God in a greater way through the expression of your sexuality?

For me, the pathway of repentance that led to freedom involved a process of stepping-stones, kind of like those required to cross a creek. As God revealed to me each step of required submission, and as I followed Him in obedience no matter how difficult, He blessed me and then led me to the next stepping-stone of submission. As I followed God in this way, chains of bondage lost their power over me and I found freedom I had never known before. These stepping-stones, all of which will be discussed in the next chapter, included confession of sin, submission to authority, undergoing therapy, attending a small group, offering restitution to those I had sinned against, and prayer. Although the process was profoundly difficult and confusing at times, and at best I fumbled along the way, often taking two steps forward and three steps back, in the end I have discovered it is the pathway of brokenness and repentance that leads to life, and there are no greater riches than the "treasures of darkness" God has stored in secret places (Isaiah 45:2-3).

As I struggled through my process of repentance, God was faithful to show me one stepping-stone of submission and obedience at a time, and I believe He will do the same thing for you. I know what God required of me, but I do not know what God is requiring of you. I do not know the current condition of your sexuality, but you do and so does God. I might be wrong, but as you read these words, I have a suspicion you already know what God might be asking of you — the stepping-stone He is placing before you as He gives you the opportunity to submit your life and your sexuality to Him in a deeper way than ever before. If I wanted to, I could provide a long list of options for you to consider; things God might ask of you concerning your sexuality; but I think it best not to. It occurs to me to leave it between you and God, and to allow Him to speak into your heart whatever He desires.

Are you willing to pray the following prayer of submission and obedience to God?

A Prayer of Submission and Obedience to God

Dear Heavenly Father, I come before you now in the precious Name of Jesus. I lay my life completely at your feet, and I pray you would cover my life with the blood of Christ. I praise you, oh God, that you are a God who can cut through bars of iron and gates of bronze. I thank you that you have stored the treasures of darkness in secret places, and I pray you would help me to find those treasures. I thank you that the same incomparably great power that raised Christ from the dead is the same power at work in my life, and I pray you would unleash the resurrection power of Christ in my life. I pray, oh God, that you would bring life to those areas of my life that have been held in places of death. I pray you would bring freedom to those places of my life that have been held in bondage. I pray you would break every bondage, stronghold, and chain of captivity that has any remaining power over me. I pray, oh God, you would clearly reveal to me any stepping-stone of submission and obedience you would ask of me in any area of my life, and I pray for your grace and mercy to help me obey. I ask that you would help me to yield to the power of the indwelling Holy Spirit and that He would render my sinful flesh powerless and inoperative. I specifically submit my sexuality to you, and I pray you would cover my sexuality with the blood of Jesus. It is my heart's desire to honor you, oh God, from this day forward with my sexuality, and I pray you would empower me to do so. I submit my physical body, my mind, my sexuality, and my penis to you, oh God. I pray you would fill me with the Holy Spirit and that you would grant unto me the gift of repentance. I pray my life is pleasing to you, and I pray my life brings maximum glory to you, oh God, and maximum insult to the kingdom of darkness. I say in the Name of Jesus that the enemy of my soul has deceived me and held me in places of captivity for long enough. I pray the light of Christ would flood every corner of my life and that any darkness would be rebuked and removed from my life. I thank you, God, that I am your child. I thank you that I do not have to manage my life solely from the basis of my own resources, but I can call upon you and you can unleash in my life your very power and resources. Thank you, oh God, for your faithfulness. Thank you that you are a capable God, that your arm is not short, and that you have provided a capable Savior. I give you all honor, glory, and praise. I say you are the only true God of my life, and I pray all these things in the Name of Jesus.

Feel free to add any words or prayers from your heart to God.

CHAPTER 11

BONDAGE BREAKERS

Building Blocks of Freedom

In this chapter, we will consider various steps that were of preeminent importance to my process of repentance. Had I not submitted to God in any one of these critical areas, my process would have stalled, and God would not have been able to lead me to the next step accordingly. Each step of my process was predicated upon my submission and obedience to the previous step. Each one of the topics we are about to consider was a building block for my freedom, and God, as the master architect knew the precise and necessary alignment of the building blocks.

I believe if God asks a step of obedience of you, and you refuse to take that step, God does not let you get away with it. He will not allow you to bypass that step and then allow the process of your healing and freedom to proceed accordingly. Before you get to step five, you have to successfully complete step four. But before you get to step four, you have to successfully complete step three, and so on. Your freedom and redemption will be based upon your complete and absolute submission and obedience to God in everything He reveals and requires of you, no matter how small, irrelevant, impossible, or painful it may seem. There is only one way to freedom and victory, and that is God's way. You will either follow Him in every step He places before your path, or you will not.

It is profoundly difficult to succinctly write about each one of the following topics, as each is worthy of an entire book. Consider these introductory comments on each topic; determine how they might apply to you and what God might be asking of you.

1. Confession of Sin

The significance of this important topic in my healing process seems almost impossible to convey with the inadequate tool of words. Yet confession of my sin, both to God and to others, became of preeminent importance to my healing process. As God began the mysterious process of redeeming my sexuality and my life after so many years of sin, failure, and pain, one of the first things He required of me was confession of sin. For so many years I struggled alone. Nobody really knew the depth of my struggle, sin, or failure, and nobody knew what was really going on in my life. I always carefully maintained my "good Christian guy" image to the best of my ability in the Christian community in which I lived, and like Adam, I used bushes to hide the naked reality of my life. I intuitively knew that exposure of who I really was and what I really struggled with would lead to shame, so I was careful to keep myself hidden. I'm convinced this is one of the devil's primary strategies to keep "Warrior Poets" in places of captivity as "Prisoners of War," as he isolates us into fighting our toughest battles alone. Because of his deception, coupled with our natural inclination to hide our failures, we can easily convince ourselves that we have our sin under control and we are capable of managing our problems on our own, when in fact we are seriously in need of help from others. It's so easy to rationalize to ourselves and minimize our sin by telling ourselves things like: "I know I've been struggling with this area of my life for a long time, but I am really going to try hard, and I am going to get it together. I don't think I need to tell anybody else about it, because they probably wouldn't understand, and they would think less of me. Besides, I stand before God, and I answer to Him. I don't have to tell other people about my struggles. It's none of their business anyway. Besides, every guy at church has issues."

Of course, it's one thing to deal with our sin and our struggles privately before God as He works in our lives to make us more like Jesus. It's quite another thing to continue struggling alone with sinful patterns and bondages that have held us captive for years and that have defeated our lives repeatedly. Sooner or later we must come to the place of admitting the truth and acknowledging that we are not in control of our sin, but that our sin is in control of us; that we have a serious problem that is really bigger than we have wanted to admit, and that we need someone else's help. My understanding is, according to most twelve-step programs, this is the very first step necessary to the healing process: a person must be willing to admit to himself and then to others that he has a problem he cannot handle.

If you are struggling, like I was for so long, to find freedom from the sexual sin, or any other sin for that matter, that holds you captive, I beg you to please believe the truth of this principle and to prayerfully consider finding a Christian friend — someone you respect and trust — and confess your sin and your struggle. The Christian church is a community of struggling believers, and we all desperately need one another. Do not continue to fight your battle alone. Do not continue to live a lie. Use wisdom and discretion. Confession of sin does not mean you should indiscriminately blab your sins to everyone and anyone who will listen, but realize you must move into the light if you want to break the power of sin in your life and find the true freedom God wants to give you. I wish I could tell you there is another easier way to find freedom, but there is not. I am convinced that confession is an indispensable and necessary step to real freedom. We must come to the place where we are willing to admit the truth to ourselves first, then to God, and then to another trusted person. Although the truth is an incredibly hard master to face when it calls our name and demands our obedience, it ultimately simplifies every struggle and makes freedom possible.

> If we confess our sins, he is faithful and just and will forgive us our sins and purify us from all unrighteousness. I John 1:9

> Carry each other's burdens, and in this way you will fulfill the law of Christ. Galatians 6:2

> Therefore confess your sins to each other and pray for each other so that you may be healed. The prayer of a righteous man is powerful and effective. James 5:16

Note: For more details on the topic of confession, read chapters 21 & 22 in *Stories*.

2. Submission to Authority

Another significant stepping-stone in the process of my repentance was submission to authority. As I reflect on the slow but redemptive process God began to take me through; a process that began on the day of my confession; I believe my willingness to submit from a broken heart of humility and destitution to the guidance of my spiritual authorities was significant to my healing process. I was so overwhelmed at the time because my marriage was in crisis and I was coming face-to-face for the first time with the reality that my sin was bigger than me. For years I had attempted to manage my sin to the best of my ability and somehow deceived myself into minimizing my sin and rationalizing to myself that it really wasn't all that bad. As I finally allowed myself to admit that my sin was bigger than me, and I saw with clarity that no matter how hard I tried I would never be able to manage my sin through the power of my own resources, I was filled with feelings of confusion, pain, and fear. I knew there was no way I could find within myself the objectivity or wisdom that would be necessary to guide my life accordingly. A dying man going into surgery doesn't tell the doctor what to do, and a man lost at sea doesn't have directions to the nearest shore. The fact that I had struggled so deeply with sexual purity for so long was evidence enough that I was incapable of making right decisions on my own and proof that I needed others to help and guide me at this point in my life.

Of course, I felt that I could submit my life to my pastors' guidance because not only had I known these wise men for years and considered them my friends, but I also deeply sensed their love and believed they genuinely cared for me and my family. It was not that I intended to abdicate the responsibility of my life to these men, as if they would then formulate every decision on my behalf and determine the direction and future of my life; nor would it be their intention to commandeer my life by somehow forcibly seizing control and then pontificating to me their opinions and requiring my blind obedience regardless of my thoughts or feelings. My intuition simply told me the best thing I could do, given my circumstances, was to surrender and submit completely to the recommendation and guidance of my God-given spiritual authorities. For the first time I knew I was incapable of managing my problem alone, and the best thing I could do to start over and have any hope of rebuilding my life was to submit to the loving guidance of others more objective and wiser than me.

Although this kind of dependence on others may appear as weakness in the world's eyes, I believe it is a strength when considered from the values of God's economy. In fact, I think my stubborn and autonomous heart, insistent on maintaining the illusion of control and demanding its own way for so many years, only delayed God's healing process in my life. It was only when I finally came to a kind of end of myself — in large part due to the impossible circumstances I had created — that I recognized how desperately I needed others' help. Only then was God finally able to move into my life and begin His handiwork. I believe submission to authority provides great strength and blessing; it is not a place of weakness, loss of control, or bondage, as the devil would lie to us and want us to believe.

The Bible teaches that God's ultimate authority is expressed throughout the earth via an intricate system of delegated, God-instituted authorities. These ordained systems of God's authority include the home (Ephesians 5:21-6:4), the workplace (Ephesians 6:5-9), the society and government (Romans 13:1-7), and the Church (Hebrews 13:17; Acts 20:28; I Timothy 3:1-13). God has established these systems of delegated authority in these various human institutions as a way of extending His divine authority throughout the entire earth and all of human affairs. No one is exempt from authority in his or her life, and submission to these God-ordained authorities is equivalent to submission to God Himself. In other words, one significant way to submit to God Himself is to submit to the authorities God has placed in our lives, and failing to do so is to disobey God Himself!

I'm not sure I can explain exactly how or why, but somehow God's blessing and power follows submission to authority. A child is protected from the pouring rain as he walks alongside his father and stays under the protective covering of the father's umbrella. If the child chooses to rebel against his father and run away, the child is no longer under the father's protection and is now subject to the pouring rain and all possible consequences. The child will probably get soaking wet. The child might catch a cold, get pneumonia, and even die — all because he rejected the protective covering of his father's umbrella. That's kind of how spiritual authority works; as we move back into submission to the authorities God has placed in our lives, there is a God-ordained protection and approval that results accordingly, allowing God to freely bless and work deeply in our lives. I believe this is why my submission to authority was so strategic to my healing process and eventual freedom. Submitting to my spiritual authorities was like submitting to God Himself. It was like coming in out of the rain. Submitting allowed me to move from a place of autonomy, duplicity, and darkness, to a place of dependence, truth, and light. It was God finally getting me in the place where He could begin to break the chains that had held me captive for so long. "Obey your leaders and submit to their authority. They keep watch over you as men who must give an account. Obey them so that their work will be a joy, not a burden, for that would be of no advantage to you" (Hebrews 13:17).

Note: For more details on the topic of submission, read chapter 23 in *Stories*.

3. Therapy

Before I even confessed and determined to submit to the authority and guidance of my pastors, I suspected that they would encourage me to begin meeting with a professional therapist, which was exactly what they recommended. I believed in my heart God was going to use my spiritual authorities to lead me, and since they thought this was the best thing for me to do, I agreed and complied immediately. Further, I knew I needed serious help dealing with the issues in my life, and the thought of meeting with someone who could provide this assistance seemed very appealing to me. After struggling with my problems alone for so long, I welcomed the idea of inviting others to my side who would be able to contribute to my healing process. Like a drowning man drifting in the middle of the ocean, surrounded by treacherous currents and powerful waves, I had been thrashing about in the futile attempt to rescue myself for long enough. I saw my therapist like a Coast Guard Marine equipped with life preservers and other life-saving equipment to facilitate my rescue. When I began therapy, I had no way of knowing it was going to be so involved, and I ultimately attended therapy for a total of almost 6 years, with the time being divided between two different counselors.

Although I believe my therapy was an indispensable part of my healing and freedom, it was a completely different process than I expected. I knew I had serious problems with both my sexuality and my marriage, and as a result I expected my therapy to focus on the realities of my present-day life and marriage. I tended to see my primary problem as my difficult marriage and the fact that my wife would hardly ever have sex with me. "That's my problem!" I thought. "I'm married to a woman who refuses to have sex with me, which causes me to struggle with controlling my sexuality. My real problem is my wife." But instead of focusing on these things, my therapist instead seemed intent on helping me understand the broader picture of my entire life. He helped me to see *how* I had arrived at the destination of my difficult marriage. For instance, while I saw myself at number ten on an imaginary scale, and I defined number ten as a marriage with a woman who wouldn't have sex with me, my therapist helped me realize that "number ten" does not exist alone, but numbers one through nine precede it. Thus, I learned that my marriage didn't stand alone as an isolated circumstance in my life, but was in fact a depository for the culmination of all my life experiences and the person I had become.

When I began my therapy, I failed to comprehend the broader "story" of my life and how deeply I had been affected by so many influences in my life, like pornography, the examples of masculinity provided by my father and my pastor, or the seductive women who had toyed with me. I saw those events as having happened years earlier, but not influencing the person I had become or the man my wife married. My therapist helped me with the difficult process of facing my past and slowly comprehending how these things deeply affected me as a person, influenced the development of my sexuality, and contributed to the kind of man I had become.

In the end, I began to see that the healing I was seeking wasn't about the smaller picture of my marriage, but it was about the bigger picture of my entire life and the person I was on my wedding day. It wasn't about focusing on "number ten" and trying to get it fixed, but it was more about contemplating how numbers one through nine defined my sexuality and my marriage. It wasn't about "fixing" my wife so she would have sex with me, but it was about getting myself fixed and becoming a better man so my wife would hopefully *want* to have sex with me.

Ultimately I learned that I had been asking the wrong questions for many years. I had been asking questions like, "What's wrong with my wife?" and "Why won't she have sex with me?" And it was through my therapy process that I slowly learned to ask the right questions. Questions like, "What's wrong with me?" and "What is it about me as a man that makes it difficult for my wife to receive intimacy from me or to enjoy my touch?" I then realized that God Himself was serious about doing business with me — business like helping me to see the truth and repent of my sexual bondage; helping me recognize that many of my attitudes and sexual expectations for my marriage were wrong and dishonoring to God or my wife; and showing me that He was big enough to heal my wife and my marriage if I was willing to first allow Him to begin my desperately needed healing. I highly recommend that you consider the help and guidance of a professional counselor as you continue on your own pathway of repentance. "Listen to advice and accept instruction, and in the end you will be wise" (Proverbs 19:20).

Note: For more details on the topic of therapy, read chapter 24 in *Stories*.

4. The Small Group

As part of my counseling process, I was invited to become involved in a small group that consisted of several men who were all undergoing therapy. The group was designed to provide support, encouragement, and accountability for each man as he slowly worked his way through his counseling process. In much the same way a greenhouse helps new plants to grow and become strong, the group provided an environment that was conducive to growth and change in each man as he faced the often-difficult process to which God had called him. Participating in this group allowed me to be part of a community of fellow strugglers, and my weekly involvement affirmed to me that I was not alone in my battle. Other men — just like me — were wrestling deeply with issues such as facing their past, considering their wounded sexuality, contemplating and trying to understand their sin, and struggling with their difficult marriage. Other men who could relate to my battle encouraged me weekly, and I drew strength from the group as we prayed for one another, shared our stories and our lives with one another, and held one another accountable.

In his book *Pure Desire,* pastor and author Ted Roberts conveys the importance of using small groups to help heal sexual addiction. He says:

> One of the things I try to help these men see is that they can't be strong enough to win this war alone. They need God's help in their lives more now than ever. They need to fall into His arms as never before. And they need the help of men around them to fight the battle. Hell is treating them like pawns in order to tear at God's heart, and it is time they learned how to fight back with effectiveness.[1]

> These addicts must address their sense of worthlessness at the point of their shame. They have to find a safe place where they can finally let all the secrets out — with nothing held back. Small group ministry is a critical key in this process. Without it we can never come to the place of confessing our sins to one another in order to be healed (see Jas. 5:16).[2]

I agree with these observations and believe involvement with my small group was strategic to my own healing process. I think this was true because at times I felt like an alien who had landed on a strange planet. Think of it; if an alien from another world somehow found himself on planet Earth, he would probably be confused, disoriented, and overwhelmed. He would have so much to learn because everything would be so new. He would have no idea how to operate a door, what to do with a chair, or how to put shoes on or take them off. He'd have so much to learn, and that's kind of how I felt as I began easing into my new world of honesty and repentance.

I had to learn how to function accordingly in this new realm. I had to learn how to be honest with myself even if it hurt. I had to learn to recognize my sinful tendencies in relating to others. I had to learn to feel my own heart and how to give and receive intimacy in my relationships. I had to learn to ask the right questions and how to trust God more than ever. I had to learn what to do with my pain when I could no longer medicate it with things like Baby Ruths and masturbation. I had to learn how to humble myself, how to wait on God in the darkness, and what it means to journey back toward my Father's heart. I had to learn the laws governing the new kingdom in which I had landed, and I had to learn to speak the language of the King. Of course, these are all lessons I continue to learn, but my small group was instrumental in helping me begin my new journey. As we met weekly, we were usually clumsy and awkward in our abilities to tell the truth and to share our struggles, but we had each landed in this strange new world, and with wide-eyed wonder we began our journeys. "Though one may be overpowered, two can defend themselves. A cord of three strands is not quickly broken" (Ecclesiastes 4:12).

Note: For more details on the topic of small groups, read chapter 25 in *Stories*.

5. Restitution

Another significant stepping-stone in my repentance and healing process was restitution. Restitution is a biblical principle central to the Law of Moses and is reflected numerous times throughout the Bible.

> The LORD said to Moses, "Say to the Israelites: 'When a man or woman wrongs another in any way and so is unfaithful to the LORD, that person is guilty and must confess the sin he has committed. He must make full restitution for his wrong, add one fifth to it and give it all to the person he has wronged.'" Numbers 5:5-7

> Fools mock at making amends for sin, but goodwill is found among the upright. Proverbs 14:9

> But Zacchaeus stood up and said to the Lord, "Look, Lord! Here and now I give half of my possessions to the poor, and if I have cheated anybody out of anything, I will pay back four times the amount." Jesus said to him, "Today salvation

has come to this house, because this man, too, is a son of Abraham. For the Son of Man came to seek and to save what was lost." Luke 19:8-10

One of the hard realities I had to come face-to-face with during my therapy was the reality of how deeply I had hurt many people through my sexual sin. I had deeply harmed several people over the years through the misguided and sinful expression of my sexuality, and my therapy included a discussion of how I might make restitution to those whom I offended.

Although I do not claim to understand it completely, I see the principle of restitution as a reflection of the coming day of God's ultimate justice in the affairs of men — a day when every valley will be raised up, every mountain and hill will be made low, every crooked place will be made straight, and every inequity will be brought into the light of truth. Every person longs for such a day of reckoning and hungers for relief from the unfairness, injustice, and abuses he or she has suffered. Something deep within the human heart spontaneously cheers when the good guy wins and the bad guy is caught and required to pay for his evil deeds. I believe this intrinsic longing within the human heart for equity is completely consistent with the just character of God Himself and reveals something of the purpose of restitution in this life. The expression of restitution allows a tangible demonstration of repentance for the offender and a taste of heaven's future banquet of justice for the offended. As I contemplated these things and realized the truth of this principle in God's Word, I was convicted of my own need to make restitution to those whom I offended. I knew that my efforts to compensate for the losses endured at my hands would be wholly insufficient, but hoped that my gestures would indicate my heartfelt sorrow, and in some small way repay the pain I caused.

The process of restitution with these various people consisted of a variety of initiatives on my behalf, including: speaking with them face-to-face to acknowledge the harm and pain I had caused them and to demonstrate an ownership of my sin against them; apologizing for what I had done; demonstrating a willingness to understand the pain I had caused them; writing letters to them with similar themes; offering to attend counseling sessions with them to discuss the damage done; offering to pay for their counseling sessions if they wanted to attend counseling in order to expedite their healing process; and blessing them with a financial gift.

One of the important principles I learned regarding restitution is that the welfare of the offended party should be the highest priority, and the true goal of restitution is to serve the victim's ultimate good above my own. In other words, the purpose of the act of restitution is not primarily so I can feel better about myself and somehow get myself off the hook for the harm I have caused. It is to be a sincere act of love and humility designed to demonstrate a true heart of sorrow and repentance to the offended in the hope that such a gesture will contribute to their own healing process. I learned that, in fact, there are times when it would be completely inappropriate for me as the offender to initiate in any way toward the offended, because such contact from me could cause further pain and duress. In such circumstances the greatest gift I could offer is my willingness to wait in silence for the day they themselves might initiate discussion that would then be beneficial to their healing process. Throughout my counseling process we discussed the relationships in my life where restitution could be considered, and through the thoughtful guidance of my advisers determined what we believed to be the appropriate course of action, or non-action, in each of a variety of situations.

As I followed God in obedience through the process of restitution toward those whom I had so deeply hurt by my sexual sin, God greatly blessed me. Although facing those I harmed was very difficult, and seeing the consequences of my sin in the lives of others was a profoundly arduous process, God showered me with grace and mercy, and I came to understand in a much deeper way the horror of my own sin and the unsearchable wonder of God's forgiveness in my life.

Note: For more details on the topic of restitution, and a moving story of forgiveness, read chapter 30 in *Stories*.

6. Prayer

As Sheri and I were progressing through our counseling and healing processes, it often felt like we took two steps forward and three steps back. At one particular point, when things were exceptionally discouraging, our pastors decided to pray over each of us individually during a special prayer meeting. I thought this was a wonderful idea for a couple different reasons.

First, I remained convinced of the importance of submission to spiritual authority in our lives. I felt that having our pastors lay hands on us and pray over us would be significant in assuring that we were remaining directly under the mysterious protection provided by submission to our God-given authorities. I hoped that the posture of our physical bodies during such a prayer meeting — one of humility with bended knees, bowed necks, and hanging heads — would be representative of the posture of our hearts before God, our pastors, and one another, and would ensure the continued blessing and guidance of God in our lives.

Secondly, although I have always struggled with maintaining a consistent and passionate prayer life, I nevertheless believed deeply in the power of prayer. Throughout my Christian life, I witnessed two different situations involving the direct and obvious manifestation of demonic spirits, and in both situations I was absolutely amazed by the response of the demons when the Christians involved began to pray. In both situations the demons literally began to shriek, scream, and basically totally freak out in the presence of prayer. First-hand involvement in these situations had pushed my faith in the power of prayer from my head directly into my heart, and I have remained convinced to this day that most Christians tend to underestimate the significance and power at our disposal through the weapon of prayer. Thus, when our pastors said they wanted to pray over us, I was totally receptive and knew in my heart it would be a compelling and significant step for us. Of course over the years, we prayed many prayers for our marriage, and many people had also prayed on our behalf, but it seemed as if God was leading us at this time into a special season of prayer.

Since Sheri is a woman, and could understandably feel some sense of insecurity about having men pray over her regarding such personal and intimate issues as her sexuality, she was encouraged to invite a couple of her closest friends to her prayer meeting, which she did. Sheri's prayer meeting was held first and my prayer meeting was held a week later. About that same time Sheri made a trip to Dallas, Texas with our boys to visit my brother and his family.

While in Dallas, Sheri participated in a prayer meeting with several godly women who are real prayer warriors and actually have a ministry of prayer and teaching others to pray. These women met with Sheri specifically to pray over her and our marriage. Although I am not privy to the exact details of what happened in that meeting, it was apparently very powerful, and Sheri viewed it with such significance that she asked me one month later if she could return to Dallas specifically for the purpose of meeting with these women again for additional prayer. Of course, I encouraged Sheri to make such a trip, and she returned to Dallas to be prayed over again.

All together, four different significant prayer meetings happened in our lives in the space of about one month. Without really trying to set these prayer meetings up, they seemed to rather spontaneously come into our lives, confirming that God had led us into this special season of prayer. In retrospect I believe that these prayer meetings were a significant stepping-stone for God's continued work in our lives. They represented God's provision as He nurtured us through the difficult time and spiritual attack we had been under.

Another significant event that occurred revolved around a special book that God brought into my life: *The Power of a Praying Husband,* by Stormie Omartian. When Sheri returned to Dallas for her second prayer meeting, my brother sent a copy of this book back for me to read. It's a book that teaches men how to stand in their God-given position of spiritual authority in their marriage and specifically explains how to pray with and over their wives. My brother had used this book to help him pray over his wife and said it provided an effective and tangible expression of his love for her and seemed to be drawing their hearts closer. When I got the book, I immediately began to read it and felt compelled to begin praying over my wife every day like never before. In the book, Omartian provides commentary and teaching on 20 different areas of your wife's life that you can begin to pray over, a list of verses related to each particular topic, and a suggested prayer that you can pray over your wife.

As I began to use the book and pray over my wife daily for a period of weeks, I realized it was helping me progress in my God-given position of authority in my wife's life, in much the same way the "tracks" might help a train know which way it is supposed to go. The locomotive is a very powerful machine, capable of accomplishing a tremendous amount of work, but it is completely useless without tracks. All of its power and potential would be wasted. I knew in my heart that for far too long I had been squandering my God-given power and authority in my wife's life. Omartian's book helped me to find and assume my proper role, providing direction for me as I began standing in a place of power, protection, and covering over my wife.

Sheri revealed to me months later that she was very moved when I began consistently praying over her, and she sensed and believed that my prayers were more powerful and freeing in her life than the totality of all the other prayer meetings. She said she imagined that she was walking down a dark path surrounded by demons and danger, but when I was praying over her she saw me as a great warrior carrying a mighty shield and sword in front of her, giving her a tremendous sense of protection, security, and safety.

Although I cannot prove it, I believe the cumulative effect of the various prayer meetings, along with the guidance of Omartian's book and the sense of timing in which they occurred, was somehow mysteriously significant in God's unfolding plan of redemption for our lives. We had already made significant progress over the past several years as God had worked deeply in both of our hearts and our marriage. Based upon the foundation of the progress God had already achieved in each one of our hearts, it's as though He had brought us to the place where it was time for some deeper work to be accomplished in each of us through the mystery of prayer. It allowed Him to further weaken the invisible chains of bondage that were still attempting to hold us in places of darkness. Although I do not know the exact details of what happened in Sheri's prayer meetings, I know what happened in mine, and I believe our adversary's strength was seriously damaged, as the power of prayer was systematically unleashed to protect the various areas of our lives that were prayed over. In these various meetings, and with the direction of Omartian's book, our prayers included requests for the following: a spirit of repentance, a spirit of forgiveness, the breaking of bondages and curses, victory over the power of generational sin, release and freedom from sexual bondages, power against controlling and manipulative spirits and tendencies, replacement of hearts of stone with hearts of flesh, a spirit of discernment and spiritual protection, God's blessing and healing, and blessings over our future. I'm sure I won't understand the true value of all these prayers until I get to heaven, but even with the limited vision I am confined to in this life, I already know and believe they were of supreme significance. These prayers allowed me to sense a "cleanness" in our lives as if pure water had washed over and through my soul, and over my wife and marriage.

Note: For more details on the topic of prayer, read chapter 35 in *Stories*.

The Next Step

Although I do not know how these six "bondage breaker" principles speak into your life, I believe every one of them was a significant stepping-stone in my own process of repentance, redemption, and freedom. I have learned that when we are obedient to follow God in the step of submission and obedience He is placing before us, He will be faithful to bless us accordingly, and He will then lead us to the next step in the proper time. As we follow God through such a process, He is mysteriously able to bring freedom to our lives, allowing us to move into higher places of victory than we have ever known. I encourage you to listen closely to what God may be asking of you and to then obey Him accordingly.

---

1 *Pure Desire,* Ted Roberts, Regal Books, 1999, page 69.
2 Ibid., 74.

Chapter 12

Divine Desperation

100%

There's something I've noticed about God: over and over again He requires 100%!

> Jesus replied: "Love the Lord your God with all your heart and with all your soul and with all your mind." This is the first and greatest commandment. Matthew 22:37-38

> But if from there you seek the LORD your God, you will find him if you look for him with all your heart and with all your soul. Deuteronomy 4:29

> I know your deeds, that you are neither cold nor hot. I wish you were either one or the other! So, because you are lukewarm — neither hot nor cold — I am about to spit you out of my mouth. Revelation 3:15-16

> Then Jesus said to his disciples, "If anyone would come after me, he must deny himself and take up his cross and follow me. For whoever wants to save his life will lose it, but whoever loses his life for me will find it." Matthew 16:24-25

We're told we must love God with all of our heart, soul, and mind. We're told we must seek God with all of our heart. God Himself says He would rather have us hot or cold; that those who are lukewarm make Him want to vomit. We're told that if we want to follow Jesus, we must be willing to lose our very lives. It goes on and on and on! God is just so radical. When the rich young ruler asked Jesus what he must do in order to inherit eternal life, Jesus told him to sell everything he had, to give it away to the poor, and then to come and follow Him (Luke 18:22). Totally radical! One man wanted to follow Jesus but his father had just died. He asked Jesus if he could bury his father first, and then come and follow. Jesus said no. "Let the dead bury their own dead, but you go and proclaim the kingdom of God" (Luke 9:59-60). Totally radical! Another man said he would follow Jesus, but he wanted to say good-bye to his family first. Jesus told him no. "No one who puts his hand to the plow and looks back is fit for service in the kingdom of God" (Luke 9:61-62). Totally radical! God is just so radical it's amazing. If we are to know Him and walk with Him, all He requires is…everything!

The Wildness of God

One of the most surprising and unexpected things about my Christian life is how much my perception of God has changed over the years. We have a dangerous tendency to want to make God in our own image; to want Him to be how we think He should be. We want God to conveniently fit in the box we create for Him. If we say a prayer, we want God to answer our prayer how we think He should. If we have an idea or a plan, we think God should bless it and make it work. If a child gets cancer and dies, we feel confused and wonder why God allowed such a thing to happen. Such things make us uncomfortable because we like to believe that the God we serve would never allow such things to happen.

As I grew in my faith and God went to work in my life, conforming me more and more to the image of Christ, I discovered the God I thought I was serving was alarmingly different than the reality of who God really is. I slowly began to learn that Christianity is not about God understanding my life and then conforming to my plans and expectations. But that instead, it's about me coming to understand and accept God and learning to conform my plans and expectations to His. God does not live in a box. God is not responsible to conduct Himself, or the world, in a manner that is consistent with my understanding or expectations. God is God; He can do anything He wants however He wants, and He doesn't have to answer to me or to anyone else. If there is one thing I have learned since I became a Christian over 30 years ago, it is that God is radical and God is wild. I think it's very important that we recognize this fact, and that the sooner we accept it, the better off we'll be. Just how radical and wild is this God we serve?

- Surely He is not wild enough to ask you to kill one of your own children. That would be crazy! The God who lives in our box would never ask us to do such a thing. Yet that's exactly what He asked of Abraham (Genesis 22:2).
- God would never ask you to marry a prostitute, would He? That would be a crazy thing for God to make you do. Yet that's exactly what He required of Hosea (Hosea 1:2).
- Surely God would not want your adolescent child to fight an experienced warrior to the death. That would be crazy! Who would want to serve a God who would require such a thing of a child? Yet that's exactly what God had David do when he was called to fight Goliath (I Samuel 17:26).
- If you were the general of an army, God would never ask you to go into battle against thousands of your enemies with only 300 men, when you have at your disposal 32,000 troops — and on top of that arm your 300 men with the weapons of trumpets and pots. That would be crazy! You can't defeat enemies and win wars with trumpets and pots. Yet that's exactly what God had Gideon do (Judges 7).
- Surely God would never require you to have a contest with 850 prophets from another religion, and then have you kill all 850 of them when they lost the contest. What kind of God would want you to do such things? That would be crazy! Yet that's what God had Elijah do when he faced the prophets of Baal on Mount Carmel (I Kings 18:20-40).
- Surely the God we serve would never give the devil permission to kill our children, to destroy everything we own, and to strike our bodies with disease. That would be crazy! Who would want to serve a God who would allow such a thing? Yet this is exactly what God allowed Satan to do to Job (Job 1:6-2:10).
- God would never ask you to start a ministry to the people who destroyed your country, would He? That would be a hard and unreasonable thing to require, and if God tried to make you do it, you'd probably want to run the other way. Yet God required Jonah to preach to the city of Nineveh (Jonah 1:1-2).
- Surely God would never interrupt your life and ask you to quit your job, to leave your life, and become a missionary. That would be too

hard a thing to do. Surely God understands you have your own life and goals. Yet God asked Matthew, and many others, to do just that very thing (Matthew 9:9).

- Surely God would never ask you to preach a sermon, knowing that your audience would kill you at the end of the sermon. That would be crazy. It would be such a waste. Why would God require such a thing? It would make far more sense for God to let you live, because then you could keep serving Him. Surely God would not expect you to do such a thing. Yet he called Stephen to do exactly this (Acts 7).

- Surely the God we serve would never allow us to be put in prison. He would not want us to suffer like that. Surely He would protect us from such a thing. Yet He allowed his servant Peter to go to prison (Acts 12:1-5), as well as Shadrach, Meshach, and Abednego (Daniel 3).

Surely God would never require us as Christian men to surrender our sexuality to Him. God knows that would be ridiculous. He would know that we are men, that we have needs and testosterone. He would know it would be impossible to require abstinence for an extended period of time. Surely He knows it would be too difficult for us. Surely He would not require sexual purity from us, knowing we live surrounded every day by endless temptations. That would be crazy. Yet that's exactly what God required of Tony Ingrassia!

Friend, I trust you get the point. This list could go on and on and on. The God we serve is truly radical and wild! Nothing in our lives is sacred or off-limits to Him. He is God, and He can require anything of us that He so chooses, including our children, our health, our careers, our future, our plans, our finances, our very lives, or anything else He decides, including our sexuality! Sometimes the things He does make no sense, and if you insist on understanding the ways of God with your natural mind, you will either go crazy or you will end up cursing God and rejecting Him. God is God! He is radical and wild! He frequently makes no sense! He requires and expects 100% of our hearts and lives. He is completely free to do whatever He wants to do, and He does not answer to you, or to me, or to anyone else!

Divine Desperation

Another thing I've noticed about God, which is completely consistent with the fact that He is radical and wild, is that He frequently responds to desperation. In Luke 18, Jesus healed a blind beggar on the road to Jericho.

When the man heard the commotion of the crowd approaching one day, he asked what was happening, and they told him Jesus of Nazareth was passing by. When the blind man heard that it was Jesus, he began to cry out, "Jesus, Son of David, have mercy on me!" When the people in the crowd heard him calling, they scolded him and told him to be quiet, but he cried out even louder, "Jesus, Son of David, have mercy on me!" You see, this man was desperate. We know he was blind. He was no doubt poor because he was unable to work; that's why he was sitting next to the road begging for a living. He was probably filthy. He probably had no family and no place to live. He probably had no one to love him, care for him, or help him. He was accustomed to ridicule and scorn, in the same way the people scolded him for crying out for Jesus and bringing attention to himself. He was no doubt miserable, depressed, afraid, and all alone. And one thing is for sure: he was desperate! He had heard about this miracle worker, the Son of David. He had heard this man could open deaf ears, heal the lame, and give sight to the blind. When he heard of such things, no doubt his heart ached with the pain of hope that such a wonderful thing could happen to him. If only he could get his sight back. Just think of what it would mean and how it would change his life. That's why I believe he cried out with such reckless abandon when he heard it was Jesus passing by. "Wow!" He must have thought. "It's Jesus! The Son of David! The healer! The one who has the power to open blind eyes! It's Jesus!" No wonder he began to cry out with all his might, "Jesus, Son of David, have mercy on me!" You see, desperation causes us to cry out to Jesus with more reckless abandon than we have ever known and compels us to keep crying out no matter what the people around us think.

In Luke 8, a man named Jairus came to Jesus in the middle of a large crowd, fell on his knees, and begged Jesus to come to his house because his only daughter was dying there. Such behavior was way out of the ordinary for this particular man, because he was a ruler of the synagogue. He was a respected leader in the community, and no doubt he was accustomed to conducting himself in a very professional and dignified manner. Not only that, but also this Jesus was a very controversial public figure, causing quite a stir in the community since many of his teachings carried overtures of criticism toward the leaders of the synagogue. Many of Jairus' colleagues were deeply offended by this man Jesus, and Jairus must have known that his association with Jesus would have lasting consequences on his career and reputation. On this particular day, none of those things mattered; not his career, reputation, dignity, or pride; because his only daughter was dying. Jairus was desperate, and his desperation compelled him to do something he never normally would have done. He went to Jesus in the middle of the day, in the middle of a large crowd, fell down on his knees, and begged Jesus to come to his house.

In this same scripture, Luke 8, is the story of another desperate person. She was a woman who had suffered from a terrible sickness for 12 years. She had no doubt done everything possible to be healed from her disease, because it says no one was able to help her. She too had heard about the healer. And despite the frailty brought on by her disease, and despite the huge crowd that was crushing around Jesus, this little woman was determined to reach him and touch the hem of his garment. Somehow she managed to push through the crowd, no doubt empowered by her overwhelming sense of desperation as she realized that Jesus was her last and only hope for healing, and when she touched the edge of his robe, miraculously, she was instantly healed.

In all three of these situations, and in many others we could consider, these people were hopelessly desperate. They had come to the end of themselves. They had no doubt tried everything possible to help themselves, and yet their situations remained hopeless. They were each like the man mentioned at the beginning of this book who slipped and fell overboard in the middle of the night: icy cold water, no life preserver, no one to help, and hundreds of miles from the nearest shore. They were each in a desperate dilemma. They were each hopelessly lost and in need of a savior to do for them what they could never do for themselves.

And guess what Jesus did? In all three situations, Jesus responded to their desperation. When Jesus heard the desperate cry of the blind man, He stopped and ordered the man to be brought to Him.

"What do you want me to do for you?"

"Lord, I want to see," he replied (Luke 18:41).

And immediately his eyes were opened. When Jairus fell down on his knees and begged Jesus to heal his daughter, Jesus immediately followed him to his house and eventually raised his daughter from the dead. When the woman with the issue of blood touched the hem of His garment, she was instantly healed. In all three of these desperate lives, Jesus answered their hearts' desires, and Jesus did for them what they could have never done for themselves.

But remember, this is exactly the kind of thing Jesus specializes in. He came to bind up the brokenhearted, to proclaim freedom for the captives, and release from darkness for the prisoners. He came to deliver the poor, the brokenhearted, the captives, the prisoners, those who mourn and those who grieve (Isaiah 61:1-4). He came to do for people what they could never do for themselves, and that's exactly what He wants to do for you and me.

A Desperate Man Named Tony

In my personal life I too discovered that desperation became a kind of stepping-stone to the deepest work that Jesus ever did in my life. For so many years I struggled with my sexuality. I did have a sincere desire to do better, and I often tried to change my life through the power of tips, techniques, promises, and self-effort. Although I could do better through the power of self-reformation for awhile, inevitably I would fail again within a short period of time and end up back at square one. It seems my best efforts were not good enough, and no matter how hard I tried or how sincere I was I remained completely powerless in my ability to change my own heart and life. I was like a blind beggar, a man with a dying daughter, and a woman with a terrible disease. I was completely incapable of rescuing myself, and I needed someone to do for me what I could never do for myself, but the depth of my desperation hadn't really dawned on me yet.

Despite my hopeless situation, and the endless cycle of failure I was trapped in, I was not yet ready to face the truth. Instead, I continued to candy-coat my sin, to justify, rationalize, minimize, and explain why my situation really wasn't all that bad. In the end, it was my own strength, stubbornness, and pride that only delayed the redemptive ministry of Jesus in my life. I've always been a slow learner because both my head and my heart tend to be way too hard. So instead of facing the truth, admitting my depth of bondage, and crying out in utter desperation, "Jesus, Son of David, have mercy on me!", I instead rambled on for years in denial, dragging my ball and chains behind me, seeking to hide the reality of who I really was, being careful to maintain my "good Christian man" image.

So, in view of my stubborn refusal to come to the end of myself, guess what God did for me? He gave me the wonderful, glorious, precious gift of a disastrous marriage! Because He loves me so much, God engineered circumstances in my life that would faithfully and inevitably move me from places of self-dependence, rationalization, and denial to places of failure, brokenness, and utter desperation. It was through the context of my broken marriage that God was finally able to bring me to the end of myself. I tried so hard for so long to make my marriage work. I tried so hard for so long in my attempt to have my wife give me sex the way I wanted it and the way I thought it should be. And no matter what or how hard I tried, my every effort ended in failure, pain, frustration, misery, depression, heartache, and despair. In the end, in the darkest and most painful days of my life, I despaired even of life. For weeks at a time I had physical difficulty breathing. Every breath was laborious, and in a matter of time I knew I could not live much longer the way I was living. I prayed that God would kill me to put me out of my misery. I couldn't take life anymore, and I had no idea what to do.

It was from this terrible place of dark, painful, miserable despair that I found the gift of divine desperation. I was so tired of my life the way it was, something in my heart changed. I was so afraid of staying in the pain of where I was, that the pain of change seemed a welcome alternative. I figured anything would have to be better than my current state. Anything would be better than being the person I was and having my life and marriage. I began to cry out to God from a more broken and desperate place than ever before, crying, "Jesus, Son of David, have mercy on me! Help me, Jesus! Rescue me, Jesus! I need you, Jesus! I am so lost and so afraid! I am so desperate! I will do anything you ask of me, Jesus! I will go anywhere you ask of me! I do not care how hard it is! Save me, Jesus! Help me, Jesus!" And guess what happened? He heard me because He always hears a heart that is desperate and dependent on Him. It was then that He was able to finally begin His redemptive ministry of Isaiah 61 in my life; not because He was now ready, but because I was now ready. It was then that He ushered me toward the first significant stepping-stone in the process of my repentance: the confession of my sin to my pastor and my wife. The process in the days that followed would be profoundly difficult at times, but my journey began as I crossed the threshold of divine desperation.

Note: For more details on the topic of divine desperation, read chapter 20 in *Stories*.

How Desperate Are You?

Friend, I hope my testimony doesn't scare you to death. I hope your heart and your head are not as hard as mine tend to be. I hope you are willing to face the truth and learn the lessons of the Kingdom much faster than I've had to learn them. I hope my life and testimony can serve as a kind of light to help you along the pathway of your own repentance, so your pathway doesn't have to be as difficult as mine was. I hope you are willing to lay aside your rationalizations, justifications, and minimizations of your sin. I hope you are willing to hear the voice of God as He speaks into your life and that you don't run the other way, so He doesn't have to bring you a whale like he did to Jonah, or crush your foot on a wall like he did to Balaam, or use a disastrous marriage in your life like he did in mine. I hope you have the wisdom to realize that the pain of change in your life is far better than the pain of staying where you are. Ultimately, I hope you are coming to the glorious place of divine desperation. I hope something in you is realizing more clearly than ever before how desperate you really are, and that you are a man who needs a redeeming savior. I hope you are willing to surrender your self-reformations and to cry out from a dependent and broken heart, "Jesus, Son of David, have mercy on me!"

Friend, this might come as really bad news to you, but I guarantee that if you are only casual about your relationship with God, including your healing and your sexual purity, I doubt God will do anything serious in your life. Remember? He is a radical and wild God! He is a God who expects and requires 100%! But friend, there is also good news. And the good news is that if we get more serious than we have ever been about doing business with God, and if we get more desperate than we have ever been, the Jesus of Isaiah 61 will unleash His redemptive work in our hearts and lives. After all, if He can open blind eyes, raise the dead, and heal terrible diseases, He can surely rescue you! He is ready! Are you?

> But seek first his kingdom and his righteousness, and all
> these things will be given to you as well. Matthew 6:33

CHAPTER 13

THE HOLY FIRE

Cleansing Your Life

The concept that I have come to call the Holy Fire is based upon the biblical example provided by a group of believers in the city of Ephesus.

> Many of those who believed now came and openly confessed their evil deeds. A number who had practiced sorcery brought their scrolls together and burned them publicly. When they calculated the value of the scrolls, the total came to fifty thousand drachmas. Acts 19:18-19

After they believed in Jesus as their Savior, those who had practiced sorcery brought their scrolls together and burned them publicly. By making this burnt offering to the Lord before many witnesses, these believers were renouncing their old way of life, cleansing their lives of any attachments to their sinful past, and declaring their allegiance, commitment, and dependence upon the Lord Jesus Christ. It is this public statement proclaimed through fire that I refer to as the Holy Fire.

It only makes sense that someone who wants to renounce his sorcery and bring his life under the Lordship of Christ should get rid of his magical arts and books. In the same way, someone who wants to stop drinking should get rid of the alcohol in his home; someone who wants to stop smoking should get rid of his cigarettes; and someone who wants to cleanse his sexuality should get rid of his pornography and any other such items that may be dishonoring to God. That's the purpose of the Holy Fire. It will allow you, through the expression of a literal burnt offering to the Lord, to tangibly demonstrate your faith, repentance, obedience, and sincere commitment to God as you seek the cleansing and freedom of your sexuality.

In the following scripture we are told to "wash our hands" and "purify our hearts."

> Submit yourselves, then, to God. Resist the devil, and he will flee from you. Come near to God and he will come near to you. *Wash your hands,* you sinners, and *purify your hearts,* you double-minded. Grieve, mourn, and wail. Change your laughter to mourning and your joy to gloom. Humble yourselves before the Lord, and he will lift you up. James 4:7-10

This scripture has a lot of important things to say. It speaks of submitting our lives to God, of resisting the devil, and drawing near to God; three important things that we are attempting to do as we seek the cleansing of our sexuality. But, in order to do these three things, it implies that we need to experience two different kinds of cleansing: one outward and one inward. The *washing of the hands* spoken of here represents the cleansing of our outward lives. In the same way we literally wash our hands outwardly to remove the filth and dirt before we eat, we are encouraged to *wash* the hands of our lives, symbolizing the cleansing and purification of our outward lives. If you're a sorcerer, you "wash the hands" of your life by getting rid of your magical arts. If you're an alcoholic, you "wash the hands" of your life by getting rid of your alcohol. And if you're serious about sexual purity, you "wash the hands" of your life by cleansing your life of anything that is sexually dishonoring to God. The *purifying of the heart* represents the cleansing of our inward lives. The event of the Holy Fire therefore provides an opportunity to *wash our hands* outwardly, as we seek *the purification of our hearts* inwardly. Through the Holy Fire, we are given the tangible opportunity to *wash our hands* as we cleanse our sexuality and lives of all things dishonorable to God.

What to Burn

I recommend that you include in your burnt offering everything and anything that represents any form of attachment to the old and sinful expression of your sexuality. In order to do this, I recommend you include a list of your sexual failures from your past along with any other items you feel convicted by the Holy Spirit to cleanse from your life.

For the list of your sexual failures, I suggest you write a list that includes every single memory you can recall in which you expressed your sexuality in a sinful or immoral way. I know this may seem ridiculous and overwhelming to those of us who have committed so much sexual sin that it is difficult to remember it all. Of course it is completely up to you to include as much detail in your list as you feel led, but I do encourage you to be as comprehensive as possible in this exercise. At the event of the Holy Fire itself, you will be given the opportunity to place this list in the flames. As you do so, pray the blood of Jesus over it and every sin contained therein, and seek the power of God to deliver you from every stronghold, bondage, or attachment that remains in your life as a result of your sinful past. As the literal fire burns the physical list of your past failures, ask God to forever burn the power of these past experiences out of your life through the redeeming fire of the Holy Spirit. Of course, this exercise might take several extended days and many pages of paper for some to complete, but I believe it will be worthwhile when the flames of the Holy Fire consume the lists that represent our sinful pasts.

In addition to your list, you are encouraged to bring to the Holy Fire any other items that you feel convicted by the Holy Spirit to cleanse from your life. This might include any pornography in your possession, including magazines, books, photographs, videos, or pictorial playing cards; any sexual paraphernalia that was used in wrong or sinful ways, including prophylactics, sex toys, games, clothing, etc.; any secret possessions such as an old girlfriend's phone number or picture, or old love letters or gifts received in the context of a sinful relationship; or any other items that your conscience tells you are inconsistent with the new life of purity you are seeking or that are dishonoring to God in any way.

A Company of Witnesses

I recommend that you conduct your burnt offering in the presence of witnesses who will agree with and confirm your step of obedience and cleansing. Other significant spiritual life events, such as marriage and water baptism, involve making vows before God and a company of witnesses, and I believe this act of spiritual worship should be no different. Jesus said, "Whoever acknowledges me before men, I will also acknowledge him before my Father in heaven" (Matthew 10:32). There's something important about acknowledging things in our lives, not just before God, but before other men also. It brings to the event a level of accountability that will lend to its significance, not only in heaven, but in your own heart as well. In Ephesus, the group of believers made their burnt offering together. Because of this I recommend you gather a group of men who may want to participate in the event of the Holy Fire with you. If other men are not participating in the Holy Fire, I still encourage you to invite others to witness and confirm this holy event in your life. Of course, this should include people you can trust, such as your pastor or other friends, and those with a like-minded understanding and appreciation of your heart and what you are trying to accomplish through your step of obedience.

Format

The format of the Holy Fire is up to you and your friends. I recommend the following:

- Allot time for the following activities: sharing, worship, placing your offerings in the fire, and prayer.
- Conduct the event at night if possible, since darkness allows the flames of fire to dance in more vivid reality and seems to contribute to the significance of the event.
- Use a campfire kind of setting as opposed to a barbecue pit, if possible.
- Allow each participant to offer his sacrifice to the fire however he feels most comfortable, including privacy if he so desires. For example, participants can put their written lists in a paper bag or cardboard box along with any other items, and then place the bag or box in the fire without revealing the contents to the group. God knows what is in each man's offering and so does each man. Men should not be required to reveal the contents of their offerings to those present, unless they want to reveal them as an act of confession as they seek prayer, cleansing, and deliverance.
- Invest a serious level of thought and preparation to make this event something special, because it is special. You'll probably need to plan the event several days or weeks in advance, as you coordinate schedules with other men, determine whom you might want to invite as witnesses, and align details such as where, when, how, who, and what.

Prepare Your Heart

This is intended to be a holy and serious event. As already discussed, God is very serious about our sexual purity, and this event represents something awesome and holy in our relationship with God. We are seeking the healing and redemptive touch of God on our sexuality, and it is serious business. Most of us as men have failed deeply in this important area, and we are now seeking to honor God in a greater way through our sexuality. You are encouraged to prepare your heart accordingly for this event. Think about it; pray about it; prepare your list; prepare your offering; consider fasting. In the same way the believers in Ephesus demonstrated a new commitment to Christ when they publicly renounced their former manner of life by burning those things that were dishonorable to God, this event provides a tangible opportunity for us to express our sincerity to God as we seek His redemptive and healing touch. Prepare your heart to the best of your ability in humility and repentance as you allow this to be the holy event in your life it should be.

A Recent Fire

I recently had the opportunity to participate in a Holy Fire with a group of men from a local church. We had been meeting together for several months reviewing much of the material contained in this book, and it was time for us to have a Holy Fire. As the group of 12 men gathered around the fire, the presence of God was tangible, empowered by the unusual stature of these men's hearts: humble, earnest, sincere, broken, and repentant. One man played guitar, and we began the evening by singing several worship songs. The power of the Holy Spirit was present, and these men were really worshipping God from their hearts; the song lyrics were not just words coming from their heads, but were living words flowing from tender hearts. I briefly shared a few introductory thoughts and scriptures, and then one by one, each man made his offering to the fire.

Although no one was required to speak, every man felt led to share something of his story, and every man revealed what he was offering to the fire, and why: unholy lists; pornography; home-made sex tapes; dirty books; written confessions of sin; little black books; cassette tapes. As each man shared his heart and then placed his offering in the fire, we all stood in silence around the campfire and watched the flames consume each offering. Realize that these were not new men to the Church who normally sit in the back row. Many of them held respected positions of leadership in the Church. They were good men with good hearts, but men who had been struggling in secrecy to honor God with their sexuality. They were men like you and me. As the evening unfolded, we continued to share and sing. We prayed for one another, and we cried for one another. We each gave our offering to God through the flames of the Holy Fire, and I'm quite sure the strange aroma of burnt paper, leather, and plastic was pleasing in the nostrils of God. It felt unusually refreshing to experience the breath of God blowing over our repentant, vulnerable, and honest hearts. This wasn't church as usual; I felt alive. It was an awesome, powerful, and holy event for these men, just like it will be for you.

Are you willing to pray the following prayer from your heart, as a step of submission and obedience?

A PRAYER FOR THE HOLY FIRE

Heavenly Father, in the Name of Jesus I speak the following scriptures over my life.

> Many of those who believed now came and openly confessed their evil deeds. A number who had practiced sorcery brought their scrolls together and burned them publicly. When they calculated the value of the scrolls, the total came to fifty thousand drachmas. In this way the Word of the Lord spread widely and grew in power. Acts 19:18-19

> Therefore, since we are surrounded by such a great cloud of witnesses, let us throw off everything that hinders and the sin that so easily entangles, and let us run with perseverance the race marked out for us. Let us fix our eyes on Jesus, the author and perfecter of our faith, who for the joy set before him endured the cross, scorning its shame, and sat down at the right hand of the throne of God. Hebrews 12:1-2

> But he gives us more grace. That is why Scripture says: "God opposes the proud but gives grace to the humble." Submit yourselves, then, to God. Resist the devil, and he will flee from you. Come near to God and he will come near to you. Wash your hands, you sinners, and purify your hearts, you double-minded. Grieve, mourn and wail. Change your laughter to

mourning and your joy to gloom. Humble yourselves before the Lord, and he will lift you up. James 4:6-10

Have mercy on me, O God, according to your unfailing love; according to your great compassion blot out my transgressions. Wash away all my iniquity and cleanse me from my sin...Cleanse me with hyssop, and I will be clean; wash me, and I will be whiter than snow...Create in me a pure heart, O God, and renew a steadfast spirit within me...The sacrifices of God are a broken spirit; a broken and contrite heart, O God, you will not despise. Selections from Psalm 51

Jesus straightened up and asked her, "Woman, where are they? Has no one condemned you?" "No one, sir," she said. "Then neither do I condemn you," Jesus declared. "Go now and leave your life of sin." John 8:10-11

Heavenly Father, in the Name of Jesus I sacrifice to you today this burnt offering of my past sins, failures, and all these various items that represent how I have dishonored you through the wrong and sinful expression of my sexuality. I make this sacrifice to you in faith and obedience, and as a tangible expression of my repentance and my desire to walk in newness of life and freedom from the dominion of sin that has controlled my life in the past. I pray that as these flames consume and destroy these physical materials, that the flames of your Holy Spirit would consume and destroy any power, bondage, stronghold, or influence these things hold over my life. In the Name of Jesus, I submit my life completely to your power, authority, and Lordship alone and I pray that you would rebuke any and every attachment or authority these things have in my life. I pray that as this smoke rises into heaven, that the fragrance of this sacrifice would fill your nostrils and be completely pleasing to you, oh God. I pray that you would forgive me and cleanse me from each one of these items and the sins it represents as it is consumed in the flames. I renounce from my life the power of these things, and all they represent, and I pray that the blood of Jesus would completely cover my life, my past, these items, and my sexuality. I pray that as my life and home are cleansed of these items, never to return again, that my heart and soul would also be cleansed from them, never to be stained or tainted by them again.

This day, oh God, before you and these witnesses, I pray according to your Word that you would empower me by the Holy Spirit to be set free, to throw off everything that hinders and the sin that has so easily entangled me, and help me to run with perseverance the race you have marked out for me as I fix my eyes upon Jesus (Hebrews 12:1-2). I choose this day, oh God, to humble myself before you and to submit my life to you. I resist the devil and his handiwork in my life, and I pray that you would cause the devil to flee from me. My desire is to draw near to you, oh God, and I pray that you would draw near to me. In the Name of Jesus, I choose to wash my hands before you this day. I pray that just as soap and water wash away the dirt from my physical hands, that the purifying flow of the Holy Spirit would cleanse my spiritual hands from the filth, dirt, and sin of my past. I humble myself before you, Lord, and I pray that you would lift me up (James 4:6-10). I pray that you would have mercy on me, oh God, according to your unfailing love. I pray that you would blot out my transgressions according to your great compassion. I pray that you would wash away my iniquity and cleanse me from my sin. I pray that you would create a pure heart and renew a steadfast spirit within me. I offer to you this day the sacrifices of a broken spirit and a contrite heart, and I pray that my sacrifices would be acceptable to you, oh Lord (Psalm 51).

Thank you, God, for hearing my prayer and for receiving my burnt sacrifice. Thank you for doing for me what I could never do for myself. I pray that you would bring release and freedom into my life, and that you would empower me by the Holy Spirit to walk in newness of life and victory over sin as I seek to honor you and my wife from this day forward with the expression of my sexuality. In the same way Jesus told the woman taken in adultery to "go and sin no more" (John 8:11), I pray that you would help me to "go and sin no more," and I pray all these things in the mighty and powerful Name of Jesus.

Feel free to add any words or prayers from your heart to God, and feel free to invite your witnesses to pray for you and over you if they so desire.

Note: As part of your burnt offering to the Lord, you might want to pray the next prayer also as you consecrate and dedicate your sexuality and physical body to the glory of God.

A Prayer Consecrating & Dedicating my Sexuality & Physical Body to the Glory of God

Heavenly Father, in the Name of Jesus I speak the following scriptures over my life.

Flee from sexual immorality. All other sins a man commits are outside his body, but he who sins sexually sins against his own body. Do you not know that your body is a temple of the Holy Spirit, who is in you, whom you have received from God? You are not your own; you were bought at a price. Therefore honor God with your body. I Corinthians 6:18-19

Therefore, I urge you, brothers, in view of God's mercy, to offer your bodies as living sacrifices, holy and pleasing to God — this is your spiritual act of worship. Do not conform any longer to the pattern of this world, but be transformed by the renewing of your mind. Then you will be able to test and approve what God's will is — his good, pleasing and perfect will. Romans 12:1-2

Do you not know that in a race all the runners run, but only one gets the prize? Run in such a way as to get the prize. Everyone who competes in the games goes into strict training. They do it to get a crown that will not last; but we do it to get a crown that will last forever. Therefore I do not run like a man running aimlessly; I do not fight like a man beating the air. No, I beat my body and make it my slave so that after I have preached to others, I myself will not be disqualified for the prize. I Corinthians 9:24-27

So I say, live by the Spirit, and you will not gratify the desires of the sinful nature. For the sinful nature desires what is contrary to the Spirit, and the Spirit what is contrary to the sinful nature. They are in conflict with each other, so that you do not do what you want. But if you are led by the Spirit, you are not under the law. The acts of the sinful nature are obvious: sexual immorality, impurity and debauchery; idolatry and witchcraft; hatred, discord, jealousy, fits of rage, selfish ambition, dissensions, factions and envy; drunkenness, orgies, and the like. I warn you, as I did before, that those who live like this will not inherit the kingdom of God. But the fruit of the Spirit is love, joy, peace, patience, kindness, goodness, faithfulness, gentleness and self-control. Against such things there is no law. Those who belong to Christ Jesus have crucified the sinful nature with its passions and desires. Since we live by the Spirit, let us keep in step with the Spirit. Galatians 5:16-25

In the same way, count yourselves dead to sin but alive to God in Christ Jesus. Therefore do not let sin reign in your mortal body so that you obey its evil desires. Do not offer the parts of your body to sin, as instruments of wickedness, but rather offer yourselves to God, as those who have been brought from death to life; and offer the parts of your body to him as instruments of righteousness. For sin shall not be your master, because you are not under law, but under grace. Romans 6:11-14

Finally, brothers, we instructed you how to live in order to please God, as in fact you are living. Now we ask you and urge you in the Lord Jesus to do this more and more. For you know what instructions we gave you by the authority of the Lord Jesus. It is God's will that you should be sanctified: that you should avoid sexual immorality; that each of you should learn to control his own body in a way that is holy and honorable, not in passionate lust like the heathen, who do not know God; and that in this matter no one should wrong his brother or take advantage of him. The Lord will punish men for all such sins, as we have already told you and warned you. For God did not call us to be impure, but to live a holy life. Therefore, he who rejects this instruction does not reject man but God, who gives you his Holy Spirit. I Thessalonians 4:1-8

Heavenly Father, your Word makes it very clear that I am called to honor you with my physical body and my sexuality. I confess that I have dishonored you in many ways in the past through the wrong and sinful use of my body and my sexuality. It is now my desire to honor you and bring glory to you through my physical body and the expression of my sexuality. I confess to you that I am weak and powerless in this area of my life, and I desperately need your mercy and grace to help me and to empower me to do what I could never do in and of myself. In the Name of Jesus, at this moment, I consecrate and dedicate my physical body and my sexuality to you, Lord. I pray that my physical body and my sexuality would become holy vessels that bring honor and glory to God. I pray that you will forgive me and cleanse me of my past failures and sins, and enable me through the power of the Holy Spirit to bring honor to you through the very areas of my life where I have struggled and brought dishonor to you for so long. I cry out for your mercy, and I freely confess that I am unable to accomplish such an overwhelming and holy standard from the resources of my own strength. If you do not help me, Lord, then I will not be helped. If you do not save me, Lord, then I will not be saved.

I pray that Jesus would accomplish His redemptive ministry in my heart, my body, and my sexuality. I pray according to Isaiah 61 that Jesus would proclaim freedom over the areas of captivity in my life and provide release from darkness for the areas in which I have been imprisoned. You have said in your Word, Lord, that the very power that raised Christ from the dead is the very power at work in my life and body (Ephesians 1:18-23), and I pray that your resurrection power would be released in me as you bring your life and light to the areas of my life that have been dominated by death and darkness. I pray for the blood of Jesus over my life, my heart, my body, my penis, my mind, and my sexuality, and recommit all these areas of my life to you, Lord. I pray that your power and life would quicken my mortal body and enable me to live in a way that brings great glory to you and great destruction to the kingdom of darkness, as I seek to walk with you each day and honor my commitment to you through this prayer.

Oh God, I pray that you would empower me to flee from sexual immorality. I know that my body is the temple of the Holy Spirit who lives within me and that I do not belong to myself. I know that I have been bought with a price and my entire life, including my physical body, now belongs to you, Lord, and that your desire and instruction to me is that I now honor you with my body (I Corinthians 6:18-19). You have said in your Word that I should offer my body to you as a living sacrifice, which is holy and pleasing to you, Lord, and that such a sacrifice is a spiritual act of

174 THE POWER OF PURITY

worship. In the Name of Jesus I offer you my physical body today as a living sacrifice, and I pray you would receive my sacrifice as a spiritual act of worship (Romans 12:1-2). I pray you would enable me from this day forward to subject my body and my sexuality to a kind of strict training that will allow me to run the race you have set before me in such a way that I might receive a prize that will last forever. I pray you would help me, oh God, to control my body and make it my slave so I will not be disqualified for the prize you have waiting for me upon completion of the race you have set before me (I Corinthians 9:24-27).

Heavenly Father, I pray that you would enable me to live by the Spirit and to not gratify the desires of my sinful flesh. I pray against all acts of the sinful nature in my life, including sexual immorality or impurity of any kind, and I pray that I would be filled with the Holy Spirit. I ask that the fruit of the Spirit, including self-control, would be manifest in my life, and I pray that my sinful flesh along with its passions and desires would be crucified with Christ (Galatians 5:16-25). I pray, oh God, that I would be sanctified. I pray that you will help me to avoid all sexual immorality and enable me to control my body from this day forward in a way that is holy and honorable. I know, Lord, that you have not called me to be impure, but to live a holy life that is pleasing to you (I Thessalonians 4:1-8).

Heavenly Father, I give you praise for how you are working in my life and for the freedom you are providing. In my heart, Lord, I make an altar before you this day, and I consecrate and dedicate my physical body, my penis, and my sexuality as a living sacrifice to you. I pray that you would empower me, Lord, from this day forward to honor you and my wife in a way that will bring great glory to you, and I pray all these things in the Name of Jesus.

Feel free to add any words or prayers from your heart to God.

CHAPTER 14

ENEMY FIRE &
SPIRITUAL WARFARE

Be Alert

Friend, I guarantee the enemy hates what's going on in your life right now. He hates the fact that you are thinking about sexual purity. He hates the fact that his lies and deceptions are being exposed and broken. He hates the fact that you are moving toward God with humility and obedience on a pathway of repentance. He hates the fact that chains of captivity are being broken off of your life and that you are being set free. Remember? The very plan of evil is to harm the heart and throne of God by bringing maximum destruction to bear in the lives of those made in the image of God. Satan is a destroyer, and nothing would please him more than to destroy your entire life, including your marriage, your family, your children, your testimony, your ministry, your future, and your very life. And if your life is anything like mine was for a long, long time, the enemy has pretty effectively taken you out of the battle and essentially neutralized your effectiveness for God's kingdom, primarily through your wounded sexuality.

But guess what? The enemy is getting nervous because something very significant and holy is happening in your life. The light of Christ, as it floods over the horizon of a new day in your life, is chasing away the darkness. The breath of God, fresh and cool, is blowing over your life. You're beginning to wake up from a kind of slumber you've been in for a long time, and clarity is coming to your mind and your heart. There's something hungry on the inside of you: hungry for a life of significance for the Kingdom; hungry to kick evil in the face for what it has done to you and for what it has cost you; hungry to know and experience more of God than you have ever known before. You're sick and tired of being a P.O.W. and you're ready and longing to be a Warrior Poet, to rise up and accomplish the exploits God has designed for your life. You want to bring maximum glory to God and maximum insult to the devil through your life. Glory to God!

But friend, as your heart is being stirred to rise up in higher levels of freedom and victory, I want to give you a fair warning, and the warning is this: the devil is a sore loser and he does not give up easily. For a long time the enemy has held ground in your heart and life, ground he had a right to because of your sin and captivities resulting from many of the chains we have already discussed, including pornography, ungodly role models, generational sin, sexual abuse, sexual idolatry, and the flesh. But as these unholy influences in your life are being exposed and broken, the enemy knows he is losing the precious ground he has always held in your life, and he will fight to maintain it with a vengeance. Do not be naive. Be careful. To be forewarned is to be forearmed. Realize that the dragon is enraged by what is happening in your life, and he will come against you with the full fury of hell. "Then the dragon was enraged at the woman and went off to make war against the rest of her offspring — those who obey God's commandments and hold to the testimony of Jesus" (Revelation 12:17).

According to *Strong's Concordance,* this word "enraged" means "to provoke or enrage, to become exasperated, to be irritated or annoyed to the point of injudicious action, to aggravate, to have violent passion, to abhor, to regard with extreme repugnance, to loathe, to hate, to detest, to punish with anger, indignation, vengeance and wrath." It's not a pretty picture. In other words, Satan hates what God is doing in your life right now, he is aggravated to the point of violent passion against you, and he will no doubt do everything within his power to hinder the progress of your repentance. In view of the sobering reality that there is a very real enemy who is seeking to destroy our lives, we are warned accordingly by scripture to be alert and vigilant.

> Be self-controlled and alert. Your enemy the devil prowls around like a roaring lion looking for someone to devour. Resist him, standing firm in the faith, because you know that

your brothers throughout the world are undergoing the same
kind of sufferings. I Peter 5:8-9

According to *Strong's Concordance,* the word "alert" in this scripture
means "to stay awake, to keep watch, to be vigilant, to alertly watch with the
purpose of avoiding danger, to rouse or collect one's faculties from sleep or
inactivity, to raise up and take a stand." Wow! This word reminds me of
what it's like when the United States raises the terrorist alert status to code
red. In other words, we better really be alert and on the lookout, because
there is a very real enemy who is out to get us. And why do we need to
uphold this level of super vigilance? Why do we need to collect our faculties,
to stay awake, and to watch with careful attention? Because our enemy, the
devil, is prowling about looking for someone to destroy!

Friend, this is not the stuff of fairy tales. This is war. This is serious business. Be forewarned. Be on guard. Expect the enemy to counterattack your
progress as he fights to hold you in places of bondage and captivity. He will
come at you, and he will set you squarely in the gun sights of his enemy fire!
That's what he did to me.

Enemy Fire

As I continued to make progress over the stepping-stones of repentance God
was leading me through, and as I began moving in higher levels of freedom
and purity than I had ever known, I discovered firsthand the devil is a sore
loser. In what I later saw as almost laughable, the enemy came against me
over and over again in his attempt to keep me entangled in the chains that
held me in bondage for so long. What I guess he couldn't accept was that
God was doing a new thing in my life, and his old familiar tactics were no
longer effective. As a result, in a kind of desperate panic to regain the ground
he knew he was losing in my life, the evil one launched a series of counter-
attacks against me in a short period of time.

The first such attack occurred in conjunction with a piece of my rental
property. My tenant at the time was a biker kind of guy, with long hair, tat-
toos, and an apparently wild lifestyle. He was behind on his rent, and therefore, when he called me one day and said he had some money for me, I was
anxious to get it while the getting was good. Although he normally mailed
the rent check to me, he said I could stop by and pick it up if I wanted to,
and since I was going to be passing by the house later that day, I told him
I'd stop by to get it. When I did stop by later that evening, I knocked on the

door and was surprised to be greeted at the doorstep by an attractive young woman. She was wearing a very loose-fitting, low-cut blouse and obviously wasn't wearing a bra. When I told her who I was and what I was doing, she told me her boyfriend wasn't home, that she didn't know when he would be back, and that she didn't know anything about the money I was supposed to pick up. As we continued to chat about when her boyfriend might be returning, she suddenly bent over toward me, placing her hands on her knees, in a blatant attempt to let me see whatever I wanted to see. My eyes had a grandstand view of the show, and I was momentarily stunned by what had suddenly happened. I quickly realized the scene was totally uncool, pointed my eyes in another direction, stammered that I would check back later with her boyfriend, and quickly retreated to the safety of my car. Of course, I don't know for sure what her exact intentions were, or if she would have allowed anything further to happen between us had I chosen to react differently and take the bait she had so deliberately placed in front of me, but I really didn't care to know or understand her intentions. I knew I had to escape the situation as quickly as possible, and as I drove away, I immediately called Sheri to report what had happened. I sensed in my heart that I could not let the event remain unexposed, primarily because of my own weakness in this area. Further, I did not want the possibility of an ongoing temptation to lurk in my mind, or the picture of what I had momentarily seen to remain alive in my heart. I knew I had to step into the light of exposure immediately so the claws of temptation couldn't sink themselves into my flesh. When I talked to Sheri, she prayed over me immediately on the phone, rebuked the enemy of our souls, and covered me with the blood of Jesus.

A couple months later I was in a social setting with some acquaintances whom I hadn't seen in a long time. As we sat and visited for some extended period of time, their recently divorced daughter stopped by to visit. I was also acquainted with the daughter, but hadn't seen her for several years either. When she arrived, I immediately noticed that she had lost a considerable amount of weight and that she looked very attractive. I was then surprised when she greeted me with a warm embrace. As we chatted for several moments, I almost immediately sensed a sexual "vibe" all around her, and felt strange but familiar feelings of sensual energy swirl around me. After visiting for several moments, she excused herself to the other room. I completed my visit with her parents, and as I was getting ready to leave, they excused themselves to another room for several moments, and their daughter returned to greet me. She told me how nice it was to see me again, and she then extended her hand to me as if she wanted to shake my hand good-bye. As I reached for her hand, and then took it, I told her good-bye, and what happened next is a little hard to explain, but I quickly realized that she was extending a kind of invitation to me as she continued to hold my hand for several extended moments and simply wouldn't let go. My mind seemed to race ahead as the next couple moments seemed to pass in slow motion like molasses. I immediately felt the obvious presence of the "vibe," and like a lightning flash, I once again felt a sense of sensual energy swirl all around the two of us. After an awkward moment, I pulled my hand away from her and quickly made my way to the front door. After saying good-bye, I got in my car, and as I pulled out of the driveway I began to cry. Although my tears felt cleansing, they were being offered from a trembling heart that feared such a close brush with such a familiar enemy. Again, I relayed the entire event to Sheri later that same day, as I didn't want any level of temptation to be given the right to lurk secretly in the recesses of my heart or mind. Sheri prayed over me once again. Since that time I've had to push thoughts away from me on several different occasions when an invisible voice seems to remind me of this particular woman and whispers in my ear to remember her not-so-subtle invitation.

The final illustration of enemy fire I'll share is perhaps the most dangerous of all and involves a particular couple that Sheri and I are around regularly. As we got to know this particular couple it became obvious rather quickly that they struggle with some very serious issues in their marriage and that this particular woman seems exceptionally lonely and vulnerable. Over the course of time she has extended several flirtations and mildly suggestive overtures toward me, and at times I have suspected she may have some level of infatuation with me. I talked to Sheri about my feelings and suspicions regarding this particular woman, and we agreed we would keep a careful eye on her. A short time later we attended a social event that included this couple. As the evening drew to a close, and people were saying good-bye to one another, this particular woman approached me, touched me on the arm rather affectionately, and suddenly kissed me on the cheek. Of course, Sheri was right next to me, and since we had already discussed the situation, her radar was in-tune and she was immediately suspicious of the inappropriate warmth that seemed to radiate from this woman's heart toward me. This may be the most dangerous situation because life circumstances require me to be around this woman on an ongoing basis, and it's a relationship I cannot easily escape. Sheri and I have talked about this situation several times, during which I have asked Sheri and given her permission to keep a watchful eye on this woman when she is around me. Further, I have pledged to Sheri that I will do my best to either avoid or keep a watchful eye on this woman when necessary. Although this is the kind of woman who would have spelled big trouble for me years ago, as my former weakness would have been easily tempted by her apparent vulnerability, I feel a sense of safety and protection against her because of the mighty work God has accomplished in my life, and the level of honesty, communication, and accountability that now exists between Sheri and I.

A Fallen World

Although I could share several others, these are just a few examples from my life of enemy fire. We should not be naive. We are in a very real battle with a very real enemy, and he will come against us with everything he can in his attempt to defeat and destroy us. We live in a broken and fallen world and we are continuously tempted by devils and demons; seductive and vulnerable women; pornography and the instantly accessible and ever-present Internet; television and movies; magazines and books; strip clubs, prostitutes, and telephone sex; seductive advertising; seductive clothing worn by people all around us every day; immoral friends and associates inviting us to participate in their activities; the messages in much of today's music; and God knows what else. It's as if our culture has erected the false god of a giant golden penis, and our entire society is bowing down in worship. How sad! Yet you and I are called to honor God with our sexuality, to have hearts and lives of purity, and to remain clean in spite of living in such an unclean world. Although such a challenge might not be easy, it is certainly possible, because whatever God calls us to do He also equips us and empowers us to do. The Bible says God has given us, by His divine power, everything we need for life and godliness (II Peter 1:3). Yes! Real victory in our spiritual battle is very possible thanks to the very real weapons of warfare God has provided, including spiritual authority, the blood of Christ, and the Word of God.

Spiritual Authority

As the children of God, we have access to the very power and authority of Christ Himself. In the great commission, Jesus said, "All authority in heaven and on earth has been given to me. Therefore, go and make disciples of all nations…" (Matthew 28:18-19). He inextricably linked the service of His disciples to His divine authority. Do you realize what this means? It is upon the basis and foundation of His authority that we are commissioned to go forth, serve God, and accomplish exploits for the Kingdom. Awesome! We have the very authority of Christ resting on our lives, and as we learn to walk in this Kingdom authority, the power of the enemy is broken and rendered powerless. Jesus also said:

> …and on this rock I will build my church, and the gates of Hades will not overcome it. I will give you the keys to the kingdom of heaven; whatever you bind on earth will be bound in heaven, and whatever you loose on earth will be loosed in heaven. Matthew 16:18-19

In this teaching of Christ, we learn something more of spiritual authority. He has given His divine authority to the Church, we are to be on the spiritual offensive, and when the Church moves forward the gates of hell will not be able to withstand our assault. In other words, the power of the Church is mightier than the power of hell. When the Church goes on the attack, hell will retreat in failure and defeat. Light always repels the darkness, and the power of the Church will always repel the power of hell.

In Mark 6:7, Jesus sent out the disciples and specifically gave them authority over evil spirits. Later, when they returned to Jesus, the disciples marveled,

> …and said, "Lord, even the demons submit to us in your name." He replied, "I saw Satan fall like lightning from heaven. I have given you authority to trample on snakes and scorpions and to overcome all the power of the enemy; nothing will harm you. However, do not rejoice that the spirits submit to you, but rejoice that your names are written in heaven." Luke 10:17-20

In the Gospel of Matthew, there is an awesome story that reveals the absolute authority Jesus has over evil spirits.

> When he arrived at the other side in the region of the Gadarenes, two demon-possessed men coming from the tombs met him. They were so violent that no one could pass that way. "What do you want with us, Son of God?" they

shouted. "Have you come here to torture us before the appointed time?"...

The demons begged Jesus, "If you drive us out, send us into the herd of pigs."

He said to them, "Go!" Matthew 8:28-29, 31

In this amazing scripture, we see the absolute authority Jesus has over evil spirits, and it confirms the truth that Christ has disarmed the powers of hell. "And having disarmed the powers and authorities, he made a public spectacle of them, triumphing over them by the cross" (Colossians 2:15). According to *Strong's Concordance,* the word "disarmed" in this verse is an awesome word, and it means "to spoil, to divest wholly, to deprive or dispossess of authority or title, to take away, to undress or strip of clothing, to unclothe." In other words, Jesus has completely stripped the devil of his authority.

While it is true that we have a real enemy seeking to harm and destroy our lives, it is even more true that in Christ we have been given complete authority over the devil and all his cohorts. The enemy's schemes against us are powerless as we stand in our God-given position of authority as the children of God. Praise God!

The Blood of Christ

The power of blood to reestablish mankind in proper standing with God, and as the basis of victory over Satan and evil, was evident from the very beginning of humanity. When Adam and Eve sinned, God announced a curse upon the devil in Genesis 3:15, promising that eventually the seed of the woman, Christ, would crush the head of the serpent, Satan. From the very beginning of time God determined that through Christ He would defeat the rebellion of Satan and ultimately bring all things in heaven and earth full circle back into submission to His absolute divine authority. Immediately after the pronouncement of this curse upon the devil, we get our first glimpse of how God will ultimately crush the head of evil through Jesus Christ. "For Adam also and for his wife did the LORD God make coats of skins, and clothed them" (Genesis 3:21). In response to mankind's sin and separation from God, the Lord God made coats of skins to cover man's nakedness and shame. This is the very first type of Christ in the Bible, and represents God's intended solution for the dilemma of sin and evil: the spilling of an innocent's blood. This is the very first record of death in the

Bible. In response to Satan's evil assault and man's desperate dilemma, God chose to kill an innocent animal, and through the shed blood of that sacrifice, God provided the first covering for mankind's sin. Through this first provision of God, we see a glimpse of the truth that through the shedding of blood God would eventually crush the head of Satan and redeem mankind back to Himself. It is the power of the shed blood of Christ, the innocent Lamb of God, that ultimately defeats the power of evil. And it is the shed blood of Christ alone that gives us right standing with God through faith, that covers our lives as the children of God, and empowers us to overcome every assault of the evil one on our lives. There is power in the blood over Satan, and if you are a Christian, you are under the blood of Christ!

The power of blood to rescue God's children from evil and the judgment of God is further revealed through the Exodus. God's children had been in the bondage of slavery in Egypt for over 400 years, and through the leadership of Moses, God was now going to deliver them to freedom. On the night of the Passover, God told His people to kill a male lamb without defect, and to sprinkle the blood of the lamb on the doorframes of their houses. "The blood will be a sign for you on the houses where you are; and when I see the blood, I will pass over you. No destructive plague will touch you when I strike Egypt" (Exodus 12:13). When the angel of death came through Egypt later that night, he struck down all the firstborn children in Egypt, but passed over every house that was covered by the blood of the lamb. Glory to God! There is power in the blood to deliver God's children from evil and judgment. In this scripture, the bondage of slavery in Egypt represents our lives before we trusted Jesus. We were in slavery and bondage. But when Jesus came into our lives, and because we were covered with His blood, God gained the power to save us from judgment, to deliver us from evil, and to bring us from places of bondage to places of freedom. Praise God for the power of the blood!

In Revelation 12, we are given a kind of overview of the great cosmic conflict: the clash of good versus evil. It speaks of Satan's grand rebellion and how he provoked one-third of the angels in heaven to join him in his quest to overthrow the throne of God. It details the ensuing warfare in heaven where Michael and his angels fought the dragon and his angels. It further reveals that Satan and his demons were vomited from heaven and hurled to the earth, that the devil is now filled with fury because he knows his time is short, and that he is now intent on making war with those who would obey the commands of God. Like a portal, this alarming passage allows us a glimpse into the reality and intensity of the great cosmic conflict that is raging around our lives every day. And it is further alarming to realize that our very lives are at the center of this conflict. As mentioned before, Satan would love nothing more than to harm the heart of God by destroying our lives and holding us in ongoing places of bondage and captivity. But guess what? At the very center of this passage is a promise that reveals the key to our assured victory over this raging, insane, and furious dragon. "They overcame him by the blood of the Lamb and by the word of their testimony; they did not love their lives so much as to shrink from death" (Revelation 12:11). Glory to God! The way to overcome the enemy in our lives is not through tips, techniques, self-effort, or religion. The key to overcoming is in the blood of the Lamb and the word of our testimony! It is the blood that gives us right standing with God! It is the blood that empowers us to overcome evil and temptation! It is the blood that breaks chains and bondages in our lives! It is the wonderful, glorious, precious blood of the Lamb that makes us overcomers! Praise God that the blood of Christ has all power over Satan and evil, and that we are under the blood of Christ!

I encourage you to continuously place your life under the blood. When you feel tempted or attacked by the devil, cry out to God for the blood of Jesus over your life. When you pray for your family and your marriage, cry out for the blood of Jesus over them. When you seek freedom from your captivities, a heart of repentance, or anything else from the hand of God, cry out for the blood of Christ over your life. As you continuously sprinkle the blood of Christ over every area of your life, it will deliver you, empower you, and redeem you for the glory of God! There is power in the blood!

The Word of God

Another significant weapon we have been given to overcome Satan and evil is the Word of God. "They overcame him by the blood of the Lamb and by the word of their testimony; they did not love their lives so much as to shrink from death" (Revelation 12:11). In the same scripture that reveals the power of the blood, we are also told we overcome the evil one by the *word* of our testimony. Guys, this is really awesome, because the word "word" that is used here is the word *logos* in the Greek. It is literally the same word that speaks of Christ Himself and the written Word of God!

> In the beginning was the Word [logos], and the Word [logos] was with God, and the Word [logos] was God...The

Word [**logos**] became flesh and made his dwelling among us.
John 1:1, 14

Sanctify them by the truth; your word [**logos**] is truth.
John 17:17

For the word [**logos**] of God is living and active. Sharper
than any double-edged sword, it penetrates even to dividing
soul and spirit, joints and marrow; it judges the thoughts
and attitudes of the heart. Hebrews 4:12

Wow! The *logos* is literally Jesus and the written Word of God. And
Revelation 12:11 tells us that we can overcome Satan and evil through the
word (logos) of our testimony. In other words, the Word of God is a powerful weapon that overcomes the evil one!

When Jesus went into the wilderness, He was tempted by the devil. In
response to each of the three temptations Satan confronted Him with, Jesus
responded with the Word of God. "Jesus said to him, 'Away from me, Satan!
For it is written: 'Worship the Lord your God, and serve him only'"
(Matthew 4:4). Jesus apparently knew His scripture, and each time the devil
tempted Him, He answered with the Word of God. With the truth of God's
Word, He exposed the lie Satan was trying to tell Him. He repelled the darkness of evil with the light of truth. He didn't argue with the devil. He didn't
enter a discussion or debate with the devil. He didn't try to persuade the
devil or explain why He disagreed. He simply answered Satan with the Word
of God. The Word of God is a powerful weapon. It is the truth, it is mighty,
and it will always overcome the evil one. Praise God!

In the same way Jesus answered evil with the Word of God, we should
too. We should know our scripture just like Jesus did, and when the devil
attacks us, we should answer with the Word of God, just like Jesus did. If the
devil comes at you with temptation, quote verses to him about power over
sin. If the devil comes at you with impurity, quote verses to him about purity. If the devil tries to steal your peace, quote verses to him about peace. If
the devil tries to provoke unforgiveness or bitterness in your heart, quote
verses to him about forgiveness. Whatever lie the devil aims at you, respond
with the truth. Expose his darkness with the light of God's Word and he will
be powerless against you.

In Ephesians 6:10-18, we are told about the armor of God. We are told
that this spiritual armor will enable us to stand against the devil's schemes

and against rulers, authorities, powers of darkness, and spiritual forces of evil. The armor includes a belt, breastplate, shoes, shield, and helmet, each designed to protect us and empower us in battle. But notice the offensive weapon we are given to use in order to inflict punishment upon the enemy: the Word of God! "Take...the sword of the Spirit, which is the word of God" (Ephesians 6:17). It is the Word of God that enables us to fight effectively against the enemy. Imagine how foolish it would be for a soldier to go into battle without his weapon. Surely it is just as foolish if we as Christians are not skillfully equipped in our use of the Word of God. The Word is power, and it will cause the evil one to flee!

Friend, realize that these are only brief and introductory comments concerning the mighty weapons God has given us to help us in our spiritual battle: spiritual authority, the blood of Christ, and the Word of God. If you want a real blessing, continue to study these three topics as you prepare yourself as a more effective Warrior Poet. Yes, we are in a very real battle with a very real enemy, and we can expect to face enemy fire in the days ahead, but as we learn to skillfully employ the weaponry God has given us, we will be able to stand our ground (Ephesians 6:13).

CHAPTER 15

Holy Sex

Arise, my darling, my beautiful one, and come with me. See! The winter is past; the rains are over and gone. Flowers appear on the earth; the season of singing has come, the cooing of doves is heard in our land. The fig tree forms its early fruit; the blossoming vines spread their fragrance. Arise, come, my darling; my beautiful one, come with me. Song of Songs 2:10-13

Winter is Past

Glory to God! Don't you just love when winter passes away? Springtime, with its promise of new life, is just so awesome! It's when things move from places of barrenness and coldness to places of blossoming life and warmth. The sights, sounds, and aromas of springtime are so inviting. Flowers explode from the earth in a rainbow of colors. Blossoming vineyards produce a palette of fragrances that are enjoyed with each refreshing breath. The gray and naked trees begin to dress themselves and dance with the splendor of new life, as the cold and lifeless ground slowly transforms itself in response to basking in the sun's life-giving warmth. The cooing of doves can be heard, and as you try to absorb this explosion of life surrounding you, you sense the stirring of a new song trying to emerge from your own heart.

It's the dawning of a new day. Old things are passing away and all things are becoming new. Coldness is surrendering to warmth, and death is surrendering to new life. Springtime is here. Winter is past. And it's time to take your darling, your beautiful one, away with you.

Imagine the glory of this kind of springtime in your life. Imagine the glory of springtime in your sexuality and your relationship with your wife. Imagine the glory of winter passing away. What if God could really do these

187

things? What if He could cause life and warmth to blossom in places that have been barren and cold for so long? What if He could bring your world to life with an explosion of new sights, sounds, and fragrances, including colorful flowers for you to see, cooing doves for you to hear, and blossoming vineyards for you to smell? What if Jesus really could bind up the broken-hearted, proclaim freedom for the captives, and provide release from darkness for the prisoners? What if Jesus really could comfort those who mourn, provide for those who grieve, and replace ashes with beauty and spirits of despair with garments of praise? Would you want Him to do these things for you? Would you be willing to seek Him, follow Him, and obey Him in order to achieve these treasures in your life? I guarantee He is ready, willing, and able to do His part, if you are willing to do yours; I know because He is bringing springtime to my sexuality, my marriage, and my life.

Springtime is Come

I love springtime because of what it represents. It represents a new beginning. It represents starting over. It represents a second chance, and I am so thankful we serve a God who gives us second chances. "Then the word of the LORD came to Jonah a second time..." (Jonah 3:1). No matter how many times we have blown it, we are never beyond the reach of God's love, grace, mercy, and forgiveness. We are never beyond the ability of Jesus to rescue, deliver, and redeem. As long as there is Jesus there is hope, and there is always Jesus, so there is always hope. He alone has the power to change our lives; He alone can turn our winter into spring.

It feels impossible to convey with the inadequate tool of words the depth of sin, hurt, and disappointment that my wife and I have been through together. If we could somehow take all the pain and pile it up, I know the pile would be unbelievably huge. It would be a barren and very cold pile. I'm greatly ashamed of so many things I felt and did during the darkest and most painful days of our lives. I literally hated my wife. At times I resented her so much it was difficult for me to talk to her or even look at her. I avoided her and punished her with silence for days and even weeks at a time. I refused to sleep with her. On one wedding anniversary she wanted to watch our wedding video, and I refused because, at the time, I so despised the memory of that day that I couldn't bear the thought of watching it. For years we struggled and suffered. At times I desperately wanted out of our marriage, but I felt completely trapped. I couldn't bring myself to divorce her because of our kids. I had the deep conviction that a divorce would be profoundly disastrous to our children, and I wouldn't do that to my kids. I resented her and blamed her. I was bitter toward her. Toward the end of the darkness, I prayed that God would either kill me or kill her, because I saw death as a very reasonable alternative to the life we were living. No doubt the evil one, the master of death, was attempting to bring his handiwork to a conclusion as he worked toward the destruction of our marriage and lives. It was a kind of deep, dark, and bitter cold winter.

I'm not trying to depress you. I'm simply trying to give you a glimpse of how dark and desperate our lives really were. Why? Because you can't fully appreciate the glory of spring until you've experienced the harsh reality of a barren and cold winter. I long to inspire the hope in you that if God was big enough to rescue and redeem my broken sexuality, marriage, and life, He is big enough to rescue and redeem yours as well. I don't care how broken and desperate your sexuality, marriage, and life really are. I know that Jesus can rescue you. I know that Jesus can do for you what He did for me. I know Jesus can do for you what you can never do for yourself. I'm totally convinced that God can do His part to redeem the most broken lives and marriages — if the people involved are willing to do their parts. Nothing is too difficult for God, because He specializes in springtime!

New Sights, Sounds, & Aromas

As I followed God through the process of repentance He lovingly guided me through, the bondages and chains that held me in places of captivity for so long began to lose their power over me. The power of lust left my life. The power of masturbation was broken. My heart and my thought life changed. The way I related to other women changed. Through my repentance, the Holy Spirit severed my roots of sexual bondage, and as a result the fruit of sexual sin began to wither up and blow away. I found liberty and began moving in higher levels of freedom than I had ever known before. As I gained this new level of freedom in my life and my sexuality, and as God replaced my heart of stone with a heart of flesh, at least three wonderful and mysterious things began to change: our relationship, my wife, and our marriage bed.

As my wife became the sole object of my affection and sexual attention, she became more beautiful and precious to me than ever before. It's as if my confession of sin and repentance brought a purity and cleanness to my life that, in turn, mystically brought with it God's blessing and anointing upon our marriage. It was wonderful to be living in the light of truth, to have nothing hidden and no secrets between my wife and me. It felt so clean and honest and pure. It felt like freedom, it felt holy, and it somehow brought the anointing of God's blessing to my marriage in many different ways. We began to talk more and share our hearts with one another more than ever before. We began spending more time together than we ever had. We began to go on dates every week. I began to stand in my God-given position of authority as the head and pastor of my home, and we began to pray together more consistently than we ever had before. We began to enjoy each other's company more than ever before, and at times we laughed together and even cried together. Everything about our relationship began to change, and as the coldness of winter gave way to the warmth of spring, Sheri and I became very best friends.

But guess what? Not only does the springtime of repentance bring God's blessing to change and renew your marriage, but it also brings God's blessing to change and renew your wife. In Ephesians, husbands are told to love their wives in the same way Christ loves the church, and that as we love our wives in this way they will become cleansed, holy, radiant; without stain, wrinkle or any other blemish (Ephesians 5:25-27). In a mystery, our selfless love somehow has the power to magically transform our wives into the very women God is calling them to be. Wow! As my heart and life changed through repentance, as I became the man God was calling me to be, and as I began to love my wife as Christ loves the church, she began to blossom like a flower. There was a new fragrance of beauty being released from her life. She became more beautiful, feminine, passionate, alive, and radiant than ever before. She began to have a literal "glow" about her life, and the people around her could sense more of her glory than ever before. It seems the truth of how well a man loves his wife is mysteriously and honestly reflected in the image she bears to the world.

And finally, friend, we come to the issue of holy sex. Let me simply say that in the same way the springtime of your repentance will change your marriage and your wife, it will also change the wonder of your marriage bed. The blessing and anointing of God will be released in your life in the most unexpected ways, and you will be free to give love to and receive love from one another as never before. You will no longer just have sex; you will make love. It will no longer be a body-to-body experience, but soul to soul.

Making love will become an opportunity for you to be intimately and tenderly close to your wife, to enjoy her presence and warmth, and to enjoy her as a person. Your breath will be taken away by the intrigue, mystery, and beauty of who your wife is as an image-bearer of God, and making love to her will be more about pursuing *her* as the ultimate prize rather than her body, which is made of dust and will one day fade away. Imagine the glory of holy sex! Imagine the glory of sex that is honoring to God! Imagine the glory of sex that is blessed and anointed by God! This is His will for our lives! This is His plan for our lives! It is possible! Winter is past! Springtime is come! There are stirrings of new sights, sounds, tastes, and aromas!

> How beautiful you are, my darling! Oh, how beautiful! Your eyes behind your veil are doves…Your lips are like a scarlet ribbon; your mouth is lovely. Your temples behind your veil are like the halves of a pomegranate. Your neck is like the tower of David, built with elegance; on it hang a thousand shields, all of them shields of warriors. Your two breasts are like two fawns, like twin fawns of a gazelle that browse among the lilies. Until the day breaks and the shadows flee, I will go to the mountain of myrrh and to the hill of incense. All beautiful you are, my darling; there is no flaw in you… You have stolen my heart, my sister, my bride; you have stolen my heart with one glance of your eyes, with one jewel of your necklace. How delightful is your love, my sister, my bride! How much more pleasing is your love than wine, and the fragrance of your perfume than any spice! Your lips drop sweetness as the honeycomb, my bride; milk and honey are under your tongue…Let my lover come into his garden and taste its choice fruits. Selections from Song of Songs 4

A New Beginning

For me, repentance is normally a process. It unfolds in my heart in response to a variety of influences God might choose to bring to bear in my life, in His time: a friend's words, a great sermon, a good book, a counseling session, a life crisis, or the pain of a life circumstance I cannot change. I trust this book has been a stepping-stone to help you in your process of repentance. My heart for you is that you will continue to follow the pathway God has prepared for you and that you will continue to move from darkness toward light; from deception toward truth; and from winter toward spring. My hope is that you will become the fullness of the Warrior Poet you are called to be and that your life, including your sexuality, will bring maximum glory to the only true God.

Tony Ingrassia is an author, speaker, pastor, and entrepreneur. After becoming a Christian as a teenager, he studied for ministry at Florida Bible College, where he was elected student body president and graduated in 1979. Tony earned his Master of Arts in Counseling (M.A.C.) at Covenant Theological Seminary in 2007. Tony is currently a pastor at Discovery Church in St. Peters, Missouri. He also operates Freedom Counseling Service, where he specializes in helping men who are struggling with issues of sexual purity. Tony has authored the following books concerning sexual purity: *Stories, The power of Purity,* and *The Power of Purity Workbook.*

Tony is an entrepreneur who has worked in the remodeling, real estate, and consulting industries. In 1987 he started his own remodeling company and grew it into one of the largest Midwest companies of its kind. After selling that company in 1996, he authored various programs designed to help other home remodeling companies improve their business processes and increase their profits.

Tony lives in St. Charles, Missouri with his wife and their three sons. He owns a farm in northern Missouri, which allows him to pursue his other interests, including hunting, fishing, and enjoying the great outdoors.

Tony can be contacted for further information through his website:

www.powerofpurity.org

Helping Men Honor God
Through Sexual Purity

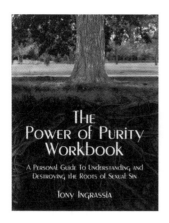

The Power of Purity Workbook: A Personal Guide to Understanding and Destroying the Roots of Sexual Sin

There's a saying that the definition of *football* is: 22 men who desperately need rest, playing a game in front of 50,000 men who desperately need exercise! This definition reminds me of Christianity because Christianity is not designed as a spectator sport. God intends for every man to "get in the game," and that is the very purpose of *The Power of Purity Workbook*. It's not good enough to just read books about sexual purity. It's not good enough to just read books or attend conferences about sexual purity. Although these are good initiatives, ultimately each man needs to "get in the game" and begin to apply the principles of sexual freedom to his own life and walk the pathway of repentance God has designed for him. This workbook provides a man, or preferably a small group of men, a practical and tangible way to apply the principles of sexual freedom to their very own lives. *The Power of Purity Workbook* will walk men through the step-by-step process of repentance that will release the power of God into their lives to bring the freedom, release, and healing they are seeking.

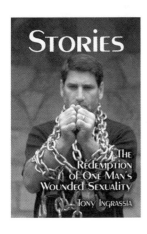

Stories: The Redemption of One Man's Wounded Sexuality

There is no greater issue central to manhood, or to masculinity, than the subject of sexuality. The relevance of this issue and the struggle it represents in the lives of many Christian men are almost universal, yet it remains one of the most neglected and avoided topics of discussion, especially in the Church. With our society relentlessly proclaiming the "gospel of sex," like propaganda blaring over the loudspeakers at a concentration camp, is it any wonder many Christian men struggle to control and express their sexuality in a way that is honoring to God?

In *Stories*, Tony Ingrassia shares his personal story of sexual struggle, sin, failure, pain, repentance, and redemption. Through the primary vehicle of Tony's wounded sexuality, evil literally tried to destroy everything of significance in Tony's life, including his marriage, family, testimony, ministry, finances, and his very life. This is a brutally honest story that will inspire the hope that God really can "bind up the brokenhearted, proclaim freedom for the captives, and bring release from darkness for those who are in prison" (Isaiah 61:1). *Stories* is a unique book designed to help men in their struggle with this challenging area of life, to help women better understand the men in their lives, and to speak into the deepest places of the reader's heart as he finds greater freedom and redemption in his life, his marriage, and his sexuality.